the SELF and the EGO in PSYCHOTHERAPY

the

SELF and

the EGO in

PSYCHOTHERAPY

N. Gregory Hamilton

JASON ARONSON INC.

Northvale, New Jersey
London

This book was set in 11 pt. Goudy Oldstyle by AeroType, Inc., of Amherst, New Hampshire, and printed and bound by Book-mart Press of North Bergen, New Jersey.

10 9 8 7 6 5 4 3 2 1

Library of Congress Cataloging-in-Publication Data

Hamilton, N. Gregory.
    The self and the ego in psychotherapy / N. Gregory Hamilton.
        p. cm.
    Includes bibliographical references and index.
    ISBN 1-56821-659-9 (alk. paper)
    1. Object relations (Psychoanalysis) 2. Psychotherapy. 3. Self psychology. 4. Ego (Psychology) I. Title.
    [DNLM: 1. Object Attachment. 2. Psychotherapy—methods. 3. Ego.
    WM 460.5.02 H219sd 1996]
    RC489.O25H36 1996
    616.89'14—dc20
    DNLM/DLC
    for Library of Congress   95-39263

Manufactured in the United States of America. Jason Aronson Inc. offers books and cassettes. For information and catalog write to Jason Aronson Inc., 230 Livingston Street, Northvale, New Jersey 07647.

For my wife,
Catherine Ann Hamilton

Contents

Contents

Introduction

In addition to a method and a technique, therapists bring to their work a sense of who they are and who the patient is and may become. How therapists see people and think about them can affect each patient differently, subtly yet deeply. A clinician's concepts are more than concepts: into them are blended personal attitudes toward others. The understanding of how people internalize and externalize their relationships, which has come to be called object relations theory, is just such a blend of concepts and personal attitudes.

In this book I introduce a new approach to object relations theory and therapy by describing changing interpretations for two concepts, *self* and *ego*. These words not only differ denotatively, they connote distinct yet complementary attitudes toward people and relationships. Numerous clinical examples illustrate what these words have to do with people, their problems, and the ways therapists help them.

In a previous book, *Self and Others* (Hamilton 1988), I discussed object relations theory as clearly as I could at the time without adding to or changing it appreciably, except in the sense that discussing ideas in new words inevitably alters them. Unlike *Self and Others*, however, in this book I deliberately change clinical theory. Building on previous work, primarily that of Fairbairn (1954), but also of Winnicott (1953, 1965), Bion (1962), Kohut (1971), Kernberg (1976), Grotstein (1981), Rinsley (1982), Ogden (1986), Horowitz (1991, 1992), and others, I contrast my new approach with ego psychology, which emphasizes channeling drives, and self psychology, with its exclusive focus on two-person empathic relationships. While illustrating some shortcomings of both ego and self psychology, the book's argument cannot help but draw upon their richness and incorporate their concepts.

The ideas developed in *The Self and the Ego in Psychotherapy* add to and change previous object relations theory in four ways:

1. They reintroduce formal ego functioning into relationships, rather than insinuating relationships into ego functioning.
2. They describe relationship patterns as they arise in therapy without searching for hidden primordial, unitary, or divided states of being.
3. They suggest that the self and the ego fluctuate in tandem from moment to moment and hour to hour, even in mature individuals, to a much greater extent than many people care to acknowledge.
4. They recognize that self and ego evolve throughout life in continuing, fluid dialogues.

Historically and philosophically, the concept of ego as a structured set of functions balancing the forces of id, superego, and external reality (Hartmann 1964) marks the end point of logical positivism and scientific reductionism, in that the personal warmth and richness of subjective human experience was entirely explained as the product of impersonal, mechanical forces. While providing some insight into a volitional and valuable self, this concept of ego objectified subjectivity and thereby dehumanized the human subject of study.

On the other hand, object relations theories, particularly Guntrip's (1969) version of Fairbairn's (1954) ideas, retained the idea of the self as subjective and highly personal. In the extreme extension of these ideas, self psychology (Kohut 1971) represents modern subjective relativism applied to clinical therapy. Empathy as a method of inquiry ideally suits the study of the personal self. Such an emotionally informed understanding can be compelling and powerful but can also turn into a therapeutic folie à deux that claims, "Because we two feel it, it is so."

My approach here brings together the objective and the subjective and personal. It reintroduces the notion of the ego, too long neglected, into object relations by discussing theory in clinical practice, the abstract within a process of personal growth and change. Because people become uniquely human and valuable only within relationships, I give preference to the self and relationships and consider ego functions important only in that they are part of, and serve the purposes of, the self in relation to others. Perhaps for similar reasons, clinical discussion[1] supersedes metapsychology in this book. Although theory is always an issue, only in the final chapter is it addressed at any length.

---

[1]Out of respect for the privacy of patients and colleagues, in case examples I have disguised the particulars, combined case material, and divided examples.

1

Object Relations

All people tell their stories in their own words. Mr. A became troubled in his relationships.

This 36-year-old philosophy professor complained that he felt alienated from his colleagues, friends, and wife. When talking in a group, even a small, casual gathering of friends, he became so self-conscious he sometimes forgot his line of thought. Although he usually managed to keep speaking coherently, he saw himself as incomprehensible, hidden from others by his words rather than communicating through words in an intimate or meaningful way. He thought it odd that acquaintances did not realize how distant he really was, although they did seem bored by him at times.

He had a strange feeling of trancelike disconnectedness. Although he could automatically report thoughts from times when he was alone, he had difficulty thinking in the presence of others. This pattern repeated itself early in the treatment.

Mr. A saw himself as an odd, distant person entirely hidden from and unknown by others. He considered his superficially normal actions and words as not really his, but as produced by what Winnicott (1965) would have called a false self. In his internal world, others did not see him intimately and showed only mild interest in his words. An odd dysphoria about his alienation and a sensation of numbness accompanied this trancelike neutrality.

RELATIONSHIP PATTERNS

In theoretical terms this summary of how the patient felt about himself and others can be called an "object relations unit" (Kernberg 1976, Rinsley 1978), although I prefer *experience* (Symington 1994) or pattern or constellation. *Unit* is too static and impersonal, suitable only for things and abstractions rather than for people. Object relations as patterns, along with internalizing and externalizing relationships, play prominent roles in the modern theory that has helped clinicians understand their patients in an emotionally attuned way (Gabbard 1994, Grotstein and Rinsley 1994, Hamilton 1988, 1992a, Kernberg 1984, Ogden 1986, Scharff and Scharff 1992, Sutherland 1989). Object relations theorists think of people as born into relationship and motivated primarily by the need to establish and maintain relationships (Fairbairn 1954).

These ideas derive from Fairbairn's (1954) notions of libidinal ego or exciting object (L.E.-E.O.) and antilibidinal ego or rejecting object (A.O.-R.O.). Fairbairn used these pairs to describe how the ego, by which he probably meant self (Sutherland 1989), relates to the object through feeling states of loving and longing or through being rejected and not loved. In the United States, Kernberg (1976), Masterson (1976), and Rinsley (1978) transformed Fairbairn's concepts into a description of people's intrapsychic experiences of the self, affect-drives, and objects in related constellations (Table 1–1).

Table 1–1. Object Relations

Self-Image	Affect	Object Image

Mr. A displayed the central relationship of alienated self and disinterested objects, along with a "strange feeling of trancelike disconnectedness." This patient's description of his internal life, however, revealed something beyond his feelings about himself and others not encompassed in the object relations concept. As what he thought and felt unfolded in therapy, how he thought about and dealt with these feelings also emerged.

How people think, process emotions, and relate to others has traditionally been called ego functioning. Hartmann (1964) emphasized the organizing ego capacities as differentiation, synthesis, integration, and balancing in the realms of perception, cognition, impulse control, and motor function. His definition adumbrates what neuropsychological testing now delineates in more detail, although such testing usually is not accompanied by the vitality of dynamic theory.

Mr. A demonstrated impaired ego functioning in the presence of others. He confined his speech and behavior to rote repetition of things previously thought or written or done and could not think creatively at such times. He turned his perceptions inward until self-observing became both excessive and distorted and he attended only to alienation, not to other aspects of his relatedness to self and others. Since the clinical material includes Mr. A's thinking about and dealing with feeling as well as his self–other relatedness, both can be used to describe his object relations patterns (Hamilton 1994, 1995), as in Table 1–2.

Table 1–2.   Alienated Object Relations

Self	Affect-Sensation	Object
Alienated.	Neutral, numb.	Disinterested.

Ego Functioning

Perceptions focused on self. Memory intact. Cognition limited to memory. Emotions isolated. Actions overrestrained. Modulation of self-expectation poor, focused on self-criticism.

This formulation is similar but not identical to that of Horowitz (1979, 1991, 1992), which is somewhat more cognitive and includes ego psychological description of states of mind and person schemas. In contrast, if an id, ego, superego structural model is used (Freud 1923), Mr. A's alienation can be considered an ego defense against an unacceptable combination of id impulses and superego condemnation (A. Freud 1936). From an object relations viewpoint, alienation does not defend against drive; it defends internal and external relationships against disruption.

Fortunately, Mr. A did not remain isolated in his alienated state.

> Eventually he began talking with his psychiatrist about how alone and entranced he felt right then, during sessions. He believed he could not think clearly and would never benefit from treatment because he could not participate in a genuine fashion. Paradoxically, when the therapist empathized with and understood this feeling and state of mind, the patient no longer felt so isolated and alone.

Mr. A slowly developed a new object relationship in which he felt valued by and related to another person who understood him in a meaningful way. Vibrant and genuine affects emerged. In sessions he often felt grateful, sometimes angry or annoyed, occasionally longing, and frequently playfully humorous. (His ego functioning during such times emerged as creative, flexible, and fully functional.) Slowly this new way of interacting became central to Mr. A's personality. He noticed the change most clearly after returning from a visit to his parents' isolated country estate.

> *Patient:* It's strange to be back. I'm having trouble getting going again. I don't know if you can understand me or not. I don't know. I'm not sure what I mean.
>
> *Therapist:* You do seem a bit vague and distant, like you used to much of the time.
>
> *Patient:* I get vague, like my parents. It's as if I fall under a spell when I'm around them for very long. Now I'm feeling better again, more solid. I get over it faster every time I come back. I'll really know I've changed when I can be around my family and still know I'm in touch with other people, and I'm not lost in some emotional wasteland.
>
> *Therapist:* It sounds like you have definite feelings about it.
>
> *Patient:* I get angry that my parents were so disconnected they couldn't treat me like a real person. I know it wasn't their fault, because they had their own problems, and I still care about them. But it makes me mad that it caused me so much trouble.

As he talked, he shifted from his previous alienated state to more integrated and whole object relations (Mahler et al. 1975). He felt like a real person who was important in his own right and who was mildly indignant about parents whom he cared about but experienced as emotionally neglecting or rejecting, whether or not they could do otherwise. He also felt more understood and accepted in relation to his therapist than he had earlier in the session. His ego returned to full functioning. He knew clearly what he thought and felt.

Mr. A responded well to a therapeutic approach that attended to his self-object relationships as well as to his ego functioning. Feeling understood by his therapist was a new way of feeling about others.

OBJECT RELATIONS AND EGO PSYCHOLOGY

It may be useful to contrast this object relations approach with one based on ego psychology. Early in Mr. A's treatment, the therapist had intermixed drive theory-ego psychology (Brenner 1973) with object relations theory. In ego psychology theory, sexual and aggressive impulses and drives are thought to well up from the id. The ego develops defenses and alternative channels for discharge because of superego pressures and an appreciation of external social and biological reality that often does not tolerate unmitigated drive discharge. This sophisticated yet still mechanical model thus concentrates on forces pressing up from below and meeting resistances and defenses that channel the forces into productive or maladaptive outcomes (Hamilton 1989). In such therapies, which attempt to bring drives and affects under conscious ego control, defenses are thought to be resistance that counters the goal of self-knowledge. Resistance analysis actually becomes the tool and process of making the unconscious known and of replacing id and superego with ego.

In Mr. A's case, when the therapist analyzed defenses against drive, the patient benefited somewhat from the comments and began to feel understood, but also seemed to feel more alone and less individually important, perhaps because the therapist's viewpoint implied mechanization and dehumanization. In the treatment the following events took place before the previously described visit to the family home. The dialogue below shows an ego psychological approach based on id, ego, and superego structures, an approach sometimes used early in treatment, with a contrasting object relations approach.

Patient: I worked in my study all weekend again. On Friday I wanted to go to the movies, but Julie wanted to stay home. I didn't really argue. I rented a movie for Friday night. She talked to her friend on the phone because she didn't like the film I got. Saturday and Sunday I had to work on my paper. But she got mad at me on Sunday night for ignoring her all weekend. I don't think I was particularly upset.

Therapist: How did you feel about giving in to your wife on Friday evening?

Assuming there might be some anger (stemming from aggressive impulses) in reaction to frustration of wishes (arising from libidinal drive) to be with his wife, the therapist asked the patient to focus on his affect.

Patient: I'm not sure. I was tired anyway and needed to work the next day. I don't know if I had any particular feelings about it.

Therapist: Perhaps doubting your feelings is a way of keeping them at arm's length. Maybe you have some idea how you felt, but need to doubt yourself.

The therapist here used an ego-defense model. After his direct inquiry about affects proved unproductive, he pointed out the defense of doubt as a way of isolating affect. The therapist addressed defense before id content of possible anger or aggressive sexual wishes toward someone Mr. A loved.

Patient: (*Seeming to guess at the therapist's assumption of what an appropriate feeling might be*) I suppose I could have been angry. That sounds theoretical. I'm not sure. It leaves me cold.

The patient did not become more certain when his defense of doubting his feelings was pointed out. He repeated the same defense, stating, "I'm not sure." At first glance the patient obviously defended himself by using uncertainty as a resistance. Based on a structural model of id, ego, and superego, the notion of ego defending itself against awareness of unwanted affects that are conscious manifestations of drives can entirely overlook the nature of the relationship in which the patient finds himself at the moment.

From the viewpoint of object relations presented in this book, when the therapist took into account the relationship at the moment, it was unclear whether what sounded "theoretical" to the patient was Mr. A's own hypothesis that he may have been angry or the therapist's unspoken hypothesis that the patient defended himself from his affects with doubt. When relationships are taken into account, perhaps doubt is not the ego's defense against drive but the self's *accurate* description of the tenuous and uncertain nature of its attachments, meanings, and communications.

The patient eventually gave a clear description of his current affect-sensation in the session, although the therapist had not anticipated its nature. "It leaves me cold," he said.

> *Therapist: (Deciding to shift from analyzing defenses to focusing on current feelings)* Tell me more about feeling cold.
> *Patient:* It's that same old feeling again. Cold, numb, nothing, sitting in my parents' living room, their "country estate," as they called it, looking out the front window over the marsh. They had a view of an Oregon marsh, of all things. I most often remember it foggy. November fog. Nothing. Haze. Everything the same.

The therapist at this point could have continued using an ego-psychology, drive–resistance model. He might have considered the patient's description of nothingness and drab sameness a defense against something more vital and pressing. Instead, he chose to address the here-and-now transference and countertransference, paying attention to current object relations and affects.

Therapist: When you said the possibility of being angry seemed "theoretical," did you mean my theory or yours?

Patient: My theory about what yours might be, really. Sometimes when you ask questions there's an implied answer and I can guess what your theory might be because of how you phrase the question and because I've read a lot and taken lots of tests.

Therapist: What did you conclude about my theory this time?

Patient: I wasn't sure, but you seemed to assume I was angry at my wife for not spending time with me and I was being "passive-aggressive" toward her by not spending time with her and then toward you by not telling you clearly about my feelings. But I felt like you were missing me entirely, like you didn't have any idea where I was coming from. Then I felt lost in the fog.

Therapist: When you feel you're being seen through a theory, even a bit, it seems to remind you of the fog. If I were to treat my ideas as good for you when they don't really fit, that would be like your parents insisting a marshy farm is a wholesome place for a child to grow up, while they both worked in the city and you had no one to play with for miles, were lonely, and hated it.

Patient: I didn't hate it. Anyway, if I did, I didn't know it. I didn't feel hate. The rest is true.

Therapist: What did you feel?

Here the therapist genuinely asked for more accurate information without challenging "resistance"; otherwise the patient might have felt misunderstood again.

Patient: Cold and numb, and I guess lonely.

Therapist: Oh yes, you told me. And how do you feel when I don't hear you clearly and add my own words, like "hate," when you feel "cold and numb"?

Patient: Well, I'm not sure. Just out of touch, I guess.

Therapist and patient seemed to have a productive and mutually vital interchange at this point. They worked together with energy and pleasure, attempting to understand the patient's emotional life and their mutual interaction and to give it words.

Patient: (Continuing) Yes, and a bit afraid, too. I get afraid I'll never find my way out of the haze if you can't understand me. Then I'd be alone the rest my life. *(Silence, then:)* I don't think I'm hiding anger with uncertainty, like I hypothesized you may have been hypothesizing. *(Chuckling at his elaborate wording and reflexive thinking)* Really, I think I never did know what I felt, because nobody talked about feelings in my family. How could I know? I didn't even know what the words meant.

Therapist: Yes, that makes sense.

The therapist concluded that his drive–ego defense model not only failed to overcome his patient's alienated state of mind but actually made it worse. He shifted from seeing Mr. A's words as defense against "true" unconscious affects from the id to seeing them as accurately describing Mr. A in relation to another person at the moment. If the psychiatrist had continued to use the drive–defense model, he might have thought that the patient's finding his comments unenlightening was further evidence that Mr. A isolated affect, maintained distance through alienation, and, possibly, unconsciously acted out hostility by destroying the therapy via the mechanism of making genuine and true comments seem superficial and meaningless. No matter how tactfully and patiently the therapist waited to uncover this material, he would have contributed to maintaining the patient's interpersonal alienation by staying out of emotional touch with him, ensconced in his own theories. Such an approach could have exacerbated the patient's intrapsychic isolation because the external therapy relationship, outlined in Table 1–3, would have almost exactly repeated his previous alienated object relations, outlined in Table 1–2.

Instead the therapist took the patient's emotional experience as valid. When Mr. A noticed that confrontation of defensive doubting and isolation of affect seemed "theoretical," the therapist reacted by assuming the patient not only correctly described his

Table 1–3.   Alienated Therapy Relationship

Self	Affect-Sensation	Object
Alienated. Misunderstood.	Numb, cold.	Interested in his theory or viewpoint more than in the patient.

Ego Functioning

Perceptions inward. Memory intact, excluding affects. Cognition restricted. Emotions isolated. Actions inhibited. Poor modulation of self-expectation focused on self-criticism.

intrapsychic world, but that he also accurately perceived the therapist as an external object. His understanding of the patient had been too abstract and therefore off the mark. When the therapist accepted this here-and-now reality, the relationship shifted to one in which he was able to value his patient's internal reality more highly than his own abstractions. This seemed to allow the patient's affects and object relations to move toward integrated or whole relations as depicted in Table 1–4.

Table 1–4.   Whole Object Relations

Self	Affect-Sensation	Object
Actively collaborating with the other. Confidently learning and improving.	Secure, solid. Confident, striving.	Actively collaborating. Confident in the patient's self. Valuing the patient above theories.

Ego Functioning

Perceptions accurate. Memories definite. Cognition active and discerning. Emotions emerging. Actions quietly striving. Modulation of conscience good, approving creative effort.

In the approach presented here, how the therapist sees, understands, and works with the patient becomes central to how the therapy affects the patient. Through the relationship, transference, and countertransference, people change in meaningful ways, but not by rearranging insights into defense and drive derivatives. The structural model of self–affect–sensation–object–ego functioning becomes central to understanding the patient as being and feeling and functioning in relation to others.

Although work with Mr. A progressed well after this point, the patient seemed overly uncomfortable with certain feelings, especially anger. If the therapist did not address this issue, it might indicate the therapist's collusion with the patient's disavowal of anger and create a barrier to genuine communication about aggressive aspects of intimacy. Perhaps what Langs (1980) provocatively called *lie therapy* (p. 415) would result. Reciprocally, the therapist's ignoring the patient's anger might represent an attempt on both their parts to promulgate the illusion of an all-good, totally understanding therapeutic relationship that was actually a therapeutic pretense.

The suggestion that the therapist give preference to the patient's experience over and above theory runs the danger of both therapist and patient avoiding conflict and denying aggressive feelings, particularly if the patient's "experience" is considered to be only what is conscious and acknowledged. Object relations approaches, however, need not avoid examining and dealing with disavowed conflict. Although the therapist in this instance agreed that the patient may not have had words for feeling in the first place, once he did learn the words, he still hesitated to use them when they expressed anger or even annoyance. Not having words for specific affects developed into a secondary defensive function. In object relations terms, the patient does not defend against aggressive drive, but against the possibility of relinquishing a needed relationship or experiencing it as ambivalent and therefore suspect. Not self-knowledge but the loss of customary relationships is resisted in therapy (Fairbairn 1958, Ogden 1994). These issues needed more attention later in the therapy, after a firmer working relationship developed between doctor and patient.

SHIFTING EGO FUNCTIONS

According to this object relations viewpoint, the ego is not a static structural element, a bastion of stability buffeted by id and super-ego forces. Instead, it is a fluid set of *potential functions* that shift as internal and external relationships change. Even mature people fluctuate, depending on their mood and circumstances, in their ability to think and modulate emotions, although such shifts are most easily seen in personality-disordered or traumatized individuals.

> Ms. B, an intelligent and educated woman in her mid-twenties, presented a subjective history of severe parental emotional deprivation and episodes of sexual abuse by a nonfamily member. In her late teens and early twenties, she read extensively about people with backgrounds similar to her own, some of whom eventually improved their lives through psychotherapy. After working at self-analysis, she underwent two brief cognitive therapies. She succeeded in her goal of achieving credits toward a clinical psychology degree, but when she began seeing patients, she became highly anxious and sought treatment with a third therapist.
>
> She chose this therapist because she considered him respected and "technically correct." During their first meeting, she described her history and dynamics, convincingly outlining her "narcissistic defenses" and how they arose. She

even proposed how her problems would be overcome in treatment. She sat rigidly in the chair, so anxious she could not stop talking.

During early sessions, her surface object relations could be outlined as in Table 1–5.

Table 1–5. Initial Relationship Pattern

Self	Affect-Sensation	Object
Thoughtful and intelligent, yet needing help with underlying and deep-seated deficits and personality vulnerabilities.	Anxious, restless.	Technically interested, potentially helpful therapist who does not care very much.

Ego Functioning

Perceptions focused on benign, conventional aspects of the therapy situation and an intellectualized self-perception. Memory intact, yet focused on the cognitively ordered and theoretically correct. Cognition orderly and able to deal with superficial contradiction. Emotions poorly defended against with denial of intense affect and breakthrough anxiety. Actions poorly modulated with constrained and rigid posture and impulsive and compulsive talking. Modulation of self-expectations intellectualized and ineffective.

Ms. B's obvious anxiety also implied a warded-off threatening or abandoning relationship at a deeper level.

Her therapist pointed out that she seemed to be doing the therapy by herself, the same way she had emotionally raised herself, with no one to help yet anxious and afraid she could not do it alone.

"That's right," she said. "And how can I know you will help me, because I've never experienced it?"

Many months later, she began to occasionally feel helped by the therapist to understand and accept herself, just as she had begun to feel understood and accepted by another person.

To feel understood and close to another person of course implies a certain risk, perhaps the risk that something unknown or absent will become present and close, perhaps the fear that what becomes loved will be lost. To this point, what caused her continual anxiety in therapy remained unclear, but it seemed to have something to do with closeness and distance. Her anxiety and rigidity arose from and covered over fragile ego functioning.

Ms. B grew increasingly skilled at describing her "narcissistic defenses" against feeling devalued and her "schizoid defenses" of treating others as nonpeople. She spoke of becoming preoccupied with internal fantasies or popular theories to avoid feeling pain in the event her love proved unacceptable or even harmful. She could create such formulations alone, or, more accurately, in relation to the psychoanalytic books she read. What she could not do alone, she said, and could only do with an actual, present therapist was to feel understood by another human being. As she felt closer to her therapist, she seemed even more anxious.

This anxiety could have been considered a sign of an impending breakthrough of erotic or aggressive feelings in the therapy, which threatened to overwhelm the ego. Object relations theorists and drive theory–ego psychologists agree that discussing sexual and aggressive feelings may be important. In the interpretation presented here, however, the notion that an eruption of drive in itself disturbed the patient is not central. It is the relationship disruption associated with certain feelings and ego states that is emphasized as problematic.

Ms. B looked forward to arriving at sessions. On her way into
the building one fresh spring day, as she walked in a sprightly
manner, a handsome and somewhat bold medical student
had smiled at her, looking her over from head to toe as she
entered the building. During the session, she appeared nervous and awkward, alternately tugging at her short skirt and
sitting frozen in a prim posture. She could not focus on what
to say.

Her therapist mentioned her apparent anxiety himself,
because she seemed unable to do so. She began talking about
the medical student. "I didn't even know him. I really didn't
care if he looked me over. Actually, he was kinda cute. When
my psychologist winked at me in the theater, now, that was
inappropriate. He was a nice guy, but I knew he wasn't
supposed to wink at me. Sarah didn't understand. She was
such a moralist; she went on and on about that and insisted I
report the guy, but he didn't do anything. She didn't get it
that it wasn't the sex that bothered me. It was being treated
like a thing, not being a person, when that was my only way
of being close to someone, physically. I had this craving to be
touched. I was so vulnerable. I was worthless. But he was
psychotic, and it was weird, but I was so lonely, I guess. It
was being treated like a thing by him, not the sex. I felt so
used. Uh-oh, now the cat's out of the bag. God knows how
you'll react."

When her object relations and affects shifted, her ego functioning abruptly changed from her previously orderly, abstract,
and integrated style to a jumble in which object images flowed
into one another. She talked in an impulsive, rambling way, as
if the therapist knew exactly what she meant. Actually, he had
felt confused and unable to understand whether she had engaged

in a sexual encounter with a psychotic therapist or whether something else had happened. Her assuming that her current therapist knew what she meant to say when he had no way of knowing implied a self-object confusion as well as a consolidation of object images.

During these few moments, her object relations had shifted, as delineated in Table 1–6.

Table 1–6. Fractured Object Relations

Self	Affect-Sensation	Object
Misunderstood.	Anxious, empty.	Sexually exploitive.
Confused.	Worthless, hurt.	Moralistically insensitive.
Craving contact.		Able to know her thoughts.
Vulnerable.		
Used.		
Worthless.		

Ego Functioning

Perceptions and memories jumbled. Cognition unfocused, confused. Emotions poorly modulated. Actions alternately impulsive and inhibited. Modulation of self-expectation poor, with harsh self-condemnation and ineffective rationalization.

From the viewpoint expressed in this book, Ms. B's erotic and aggressive drives did not overwhelm good ego functioning. Instead, reexperiencing certain relationships and affects shifted the ego functioning to an earlier dysfunctional modality associated with a set of internalized relationship patterns. The ego here is seen not as a fixed and stable structure that can be overwhelmed by id content, but as a set of functions that change according to the abilities that remain available in different internal and external circumstances and in various moods. The relationships, affect-sensations, and ego functioning all change together. Perhaps the patient's beginning to feel more comfortable, close, and open in the therapy made her vulnerable to activation of this chaotic and confused relationship and disorganized ego functioning.

In this welter of emotion and confusion, the therapist felt he needed to calm himself and use his own good ego functioning to help the patient reestablish some sense of orderliness. He needed security within himself to help her reengage her own potentially good ego functioning.

> *Therapist:* I believe you were beginning to feel more comfortable and open here. Then the student looking you over must have reminded you of something disturbing. But I didn't quite follow the sequence of events. Let's go over it more slowly. Is that okay?
>
> *Patient:* Sure, you see . . . *(and she launches into more rapid and hard-to-follow speech)*.

Had the therapist believed that repressed memories and associated drives led to her former stilted behavior and anxiety and that merely removing the repression would be a relief, he might have let her continue. Using the model presented here, however, he concluded that her ego functioning associated with her memories could not process what had happened in any useful way, anymore than she had been able to cope with whatever happened in the first place. Consequently he helped her slow down and reestablish good ego functioning.

> *Therapist:* Let me interrupt. Do you mind if I tell you what I understand so far and ask you some questions?
>
> *Patient:* That's fine. *(Settling back in her chair)*
>
> *Therapist:* Now let's see, you didn't really mind the student looking you over, but it reminded you of your first therapy. Did your former therapist wink at you in the theater in a way you felt was seductive?
>
> *Patient:* Yes, and I knew that wasn't right, so I quit that day. Never went back.
>
> *Therapist:* Do you feel like I'm being seductive or you might need to get away from this therapy?

Very carefully, the therapist helped her sort her self–other boundaries and her memories from her current perceptions. He assisted her potentially good ego functioning in recounting events coherently, compatible with the more mature, whole object relations functioning apparent early in treatment.

> *Patient:* No. I get scared here, but you stick pretty much with business. I think you're all right.
> *Therapist:* So who was Sarah?
> *Patient:* She was my second therapist. But she got so indignant about Tom, my first therapist. She had this thing about boundaries. She thought I should report the guy to the licensing board. But he really didn't do anything except wink. Reporting him was her thing, not mine.
> *Therapist:* And you wonder if I'll be able to pay attention to you and your issues, not mine. Is that right?
> *Patient:* Right.
> *Therapist:* Do you want to tell me about the psychotic guy?

Working along these lines, the therapist did not remove ego defenses or conduct supportive therapy in the sense of reinforcing defenses against id and superego content. He decided that the patient was repeating an overwhelming relationship and had experienced a shift in object relations and ego functioning. This experience seemed split off and kept separate from her more integrated and mature self, which she had tenaciously held onto until this point in treatment. In that the therapist performed an ego function for the patient by structuring the session until she could again do it herself, the therapy was supportive. By asking her if she wanted to discuss the disturbing memories, he acknowledged her potential autonomy and control.

If the patient could remember and discuss what had been split off and kept separate from her more mature self and ego functioning while she was actually in a more mature state of mind and in the safety of a helpful relationship that respected her autonomy, she could probably integrate this chaotic, internal, and remembered experience into her whole object relations. What had previously been a dreaded repetition would become a memory of something in the past from a more mature and competent vantage point.

> *Patient:* There was this guy next door. I don't know why my parents let me go over there. I was just a kid. It was bizarre. I get this weird feeling when I remember it. I was such a lonely little kid. I guess I was kind of seductive. It was my only way of getting attention. I don't really want to talk about it more right now.
>
> *Therapist:* How do you feel about having talked about it some?
>
> *Patient:* It's okay. It's just one of those things that happened. I guess I need to be kind of careful how I talk about it. I get so mixed up.
>
> *Therapist:* Yes, you do. But you pull out of it with a little help. We can talk about it some more later, if you'd like.

The structural model used here suggests that various object relations become available to individuals at various times and that these relationships are associated with varying ego functioning, at least in more fragile individuals and perhaps in everyone to some degree. These self–other, affect–sensation, and ego functioning constellations form relatively independent dynamic patterns. Individuals like Ms. B from time to time fall into a dysfunctional and distressing object relations experience; they stumble into a psychological pit from which they cannot extract themselves. When the therapist helped Ms. B reestablish her more mature relatedness and ego functioning, he pulled her out of the pit, not by encouraging her to replace id with ego, but by aiding her to change the nature of her internal relationships and her ability to think about herself in relation to others.

DISCUSSION

Fairbairnian object relations theory and U.S. self psychology were both reactions against drive theory-ego psychology, which was too impersonal and mechanistic for clinical purposes. While attending to personal and volitional emotional life, however, object relations theorists and self psychologists neglected formal ego functions as if they did not exist or were not important. The approach presented here reintroduces ego functioning into object relations.

When Kernberg (1976), Masterson (1976), and Rinsley (1978) inserted object relations units into ego psychology, they included self, affect-drive, and object as elements. They did not ignore the system ego, but tended to address it in a different arena. Among the three, only Kernberg coherently discussed the relationship between ego and self. Unlike Kernberg's (1982) and, before him, Jacobson's (1964) attempts to introduce internal and external relationships into the ego, however, the approach presented here reverses the movement and brings ego function into relationships.

Integrating ego functions into object relations need not imply that ego and self constitute different parts of a person, but that they describe different aspects of, or different ways of thinking about, the same thing—an individual, a whole person with importance and meaning to others. The ego can, if somewhat awkwardly, be described as the ego functioning of the self or the person. There may also be a supraordinate Self (Horowitz 1991, Horowitz and Zilberg 1983) in healthier, or even in all, individuals, consciously or unconsciously aware of the relatedness of all the potential self-object relations. For the moment, however, it is sufficient to build on existing theory by adding ego functioning to object relations and considering relationships the central element in mental life.

This formulation treats self-experience, affect-sensation, object, and ego functioning as aspects of a person's state of being-in-relationship at a point in time. It postulates that when one aspect shifts, they all shift together as a dynamic whole. This model eliminates one needless polarity between ego and self while it creates another. When object relations theory includes the system ego, this theory becomes a fully structural model itself yet is incompatible with ego psychology's structure of id, ego, and super-ego. At the same time, it revives Fairbairn's (1963, Modell 1994, Rubens 1994) suggestion that Freud's revered structural theory of 1923 should be relinquished as once but no longer useful. Discarding a widely accepted and once clinically useful theory should not be done lightly and without consideration and debate. Since all clinical theories rise or fall on their usefulness for treatment, more examples of using this approach to object relations in practice are provided in Chapter 2.

2

Object Relations Compared to Self Psychology

According to the theory of self psychology, as well as to object relations theory, people exist in relationship and internalize their relationships as they psychologically grow. Caregivers' empathic attunement allows them to understand and respond appropriately to an infant's grandiose, idealizing, and mirroring needs (Kohut 1971, 1977). Appropriate fulfillment of self-object functions culminates in children's developing a sense of cohesiveness within themselves and their interpersonal environment. Kohut (1971, Tolpin 1971) called this process *transmuting internalization*. People continue to need sustaining self-objects throughout their lives. Psychopathology emerges when empathic failures disrupt self-cohesiveness.

BRAIN INJURY AND THE EGO

Self psychology theoretically excludes the ego from consideration and explicitly limits therapist activity to self-object responsiveness and empathic attunement. The therapist in the following example at first adopted such an approach.

> Mr. C, a 39-year-old accountant, complained that he had developed increasingly occurring temper outbursts since a serious automobile accident a year earlier. During the accident, his child sustained a leg injury, which was not healing well. His wife, previously understanding and supportive, now blamed him for the accident, although both insurance companies held the other driver accountable. As marital conflict escalated, he could not concentrate at work. Recurrent nightmares disrupted his sleep. He did not remember the accident, but his neurologist assured him he had no residual brain injury. Magnetic resonance imaging of the brain proved normal.
>
> In the first session, the therapist empathized with the patient's feelings of loss and fragmentation. It seemed entirely understandable that he should experience a loss of cohesiveness.

The therapist's self psychology assumptions fit well with the clinical material. The patient's son, who must also have represented important aspects of himself, had been injured. His marriage and job were falling apart. His spouse and employer, who had once provided sustaining self-object functions for him, were growing impatient. They could no longer understand him. Recurrent dream-images of his car's physical structure being mangled and destroyed may have symbolized his losses as well as the physical trauma itself. Perhaps his temper outbursts were regressive, grandiose attempts to reestablish a sense of cohesiveness.

> Over several sessions, he reviewed similar childhood feelings of fragmentation, when his parents grew so preoccupied with

their divorce they could not attend to him. The therapist assumed that as he himself continued to fulfill a sustaining self-object function for the patient by accurately empathizing with his emotional state, a sense of cohesiveness and value as an individual in relation to others would revive in Mr. C.

Although the therapist had succeeded in helping a number of patients with this approach, this one became increasingly anxious and irritable. Perhaps the emotional closeness of empathy may somehow threaten him, the therapist thought, and tactfully withdrew emotionally to a small degree.

In response, the patient became enraged at the therapist's not helping. Perhaps an empathic lapse had stimulated his anger, so the therapist empathized with the rage, trying to make emotional contact.

Self psychology literature emphasizes that negative transference, or anger at the therapist, arises from empathic failure and the therapist must correct the error (Adler 1992).

Mr. C, however, became still more enraged when the therapist empathized with his anger, to the point of storming out of the office. In subsequent sessions, the therapist's empathizing with the patient's anger always led to increased anger, almost to dangerous anger. Mr. C did not feel calmed and reassured by understanding: empathy added fuel to the fire.

Realizing he had gone as far as he could with this approach, the therapist fortunately let common sense intercede and broke with his preferred technique.

As the patient ranted and raved during one session, the psychiatrist spontaneously said, "Mr. C, calm yourself a moment. Let's see what we can do to make things better. There are some things we can do. Take a few deep breaths, calm down, then let's think about this."

The patient immediately calmed.

After consultation, the psychiatrist referred the patient for neuropsychological testing to review ego functioning more subtly than did mental status screening, neurological examination of gross motor and sensory function, and magnetic resonance brain imaging that Mr. C had previously undergone. The patient showed marked difficulty in using recent memory and in concentrating, abstracting, and processing complex stimuli. In view of his previous educational and job performance, these deficits must have been new and were probably caused by the automobile accident.

Mr. C's object relations patterns, which incorporate ego functioning in his relationships, can now be described as in Table 2–1.

The self psychology approach that focuses on emotional experience in relation to the object is largely compatible with object relations approaches. Mr. C's therapist took steps similar to those of Mr. A's therapist as described in Chapter 1. Mr. C, however, unlike Mr. A, had organically impaired integrative ego functions, and his therapist could not conceptualize such a circumstance within self psychology. Fortunately, he intuitively shifted approaches and obtained consultation.

Mr. A, in contrast to this patient, could perform complex integrating and differentiating mental processes. When his psychiatrist empathized with his disappointment in being seen through the lens of a mechanistic theory, he could hold opposites in mind at the same time and feel understood by the same person who had misunderstood him. Once he felt understood, his potential good ego functioning automatically regained its full potential. Mr. C,

Table 2–1. Threatened, Enraged Object Relations

Self	Affect-Sensation	Object
Injured.	Enraged, tension.	Threatening.

Ego Functioning

Perceptions hyperalert. Memory intact for long-term events, impaired for recent events and time of accident. Cognition concrete, unable to process complex stimuli or to hold opposites in mind simultaneously. Emotions poorly modulated. Actions impulsive and unmodulated. Modulation of self-expectation impaired, either on or off.

however, could no longer process complex stimuli, or abstract or modulate emotions. When he felt angry, he could not respond to empathy by feeling that his therapist now understood that he had misunderstood the patient. If his therapist validated his anger by empathizing with it, Mr. C took that validation concretely, as justification for more anger. He could not reflect on his emotions or calm himself. When his therapist empathized with anxiety and fragmentation, he felt that the therapist along with himself had been overwhelmed so that nothing could be done to help him. He became more anxious.

If the therapist failed empathically in this treatment, it resulted from not realizing how frustrating it must have been for the patient to cope with information and modulate emotions. Self psychology, however, claims empathy as the only legitimate observational tool, and empathy addresses only affects and self-experience, not perceptual-motor-cognitive functions. By having no words for ego functions, self psychology severely handicaps itself in dealing with the results of brain pathology. In Mr. C's case, as long as the therapist exclusively considered self-experience, the patient deteriorated. The therapist had to break with his theory, assess impaired ego functioning, and perform some of those functions for the patient. That is, he had to move outside the patient's current subjectivity and introduce something different—calm thoughtfulness from an outside viewpoint. When the therapist performed this ego function for him, the patient could immediately calm down and accept advice, although he could not think flexibly himself.

This therapist eventually talked with Mr. C's wife about Mr. C's brain injury and discussed how to perform ego functions for her husband, how to calm him by calming herself, how to give clear direction and praise, and how to provide specific, accomplishable tasks. He eventually referred the wife to another therapist, who could empathize with her losses and her feelings about having to be so thoughtful and self-controlled with her husband. As she worked with these problems, she overcame her tendency to blame her husband and could begin her own grieving. Her husband, however, could never grieve for his losses.

As Klein and Riviere (1964) observed, grieving requires the ability to hold emotional opposites in mind at the same time, to value people and things for what they are or were and yet to remain disappointed or hurt by their current shortcoming or absence. Mr. C could not feel sad about or accept the accident or the loss of his son's and his own health and of his former professional functioning. These subjects were not to be discussed: he could only get angry. He no longer had the ego ability to hold opposites in mind at the same time, although he could remember whole object relations from the past in his long-term memory.

His therapist had to go through his own grief at the limits of his ability to help. By doing so, by using his own ego functioning to cope with disappointment, he could at least help his patient in small ways, which proved to have significant practical value for the patient and his family.

Individuals with structural brain injury and resulting neuro-psychological deficits provide a clear example of the need to attend to ego function when considering self-object relationships. Self psychology's dyadic structure of self and self-object, or even object relation theory's concept of self-affect-object, is not sufficient to ameliorate this clinical situation unless an ego concept is added.

THE FALSE SELF AND THE EGO

Not only with brain-injured individuals but on other occasions, the therapist can benefit from considering ego functioning inherent in various object relations.

> Mr. D, a 48-year-old corporate attorney, became severely depressed after his divorce. His despondency grew so great that he gave up his practice. His friends could not console him. He entered twice- and then three-times-weekly treatment with a therapist who empathized with his loss and depression.
>
> When Mr. D was a child, his mother had succumbed to depression herself and left him emotionally isolated much of the time. His father, who had suffered through the economic depression of the 1930s and the deprivations of World War II, feared poverty as the destructive force it can be. His father overworked and earned enough money to send Mr. D to a private boarding school, partly because neither parent could care for the boy and partly because both parents considered education and status more important than personal attachments. He succeeded as a student, student body leader, and caretaker of his classmates.

In self psychology terms, this patient's parents could not empathize with his vulnerability, loneliness, and need for parental support: they considered such feelings as having nothing to do with him. His mother's depression and his father's absence also interfered with his need to idealize his parents. Instead, he attempted to become his own idealized self-object, always successful, always self-sufficient, always caring for others.

This interpretation coincides with Winnicott's (1965) false-self concept. Although many authors consider Winnicott a middle school object relations theorist, he did not develop a metapsychology. Clinicians readily apply his ideas to numerous situations and often combine the false-self idea with ideas of self psychology to explain narcissism arising from emotional deprivation amid plenty. Winnicott maintains that when parents cannot sufficiently attend to a child's emotions but demand excessive compliance, the child may despair of genuine closeness and develop a false, compliant self as the only way of being close. The child thus gains an attachment at the cost of settling for a charade. The true self, angry and alone, retreats into the interior, the unconscious. This self-aspect, never having been acknowledged by others, exists apart from human contact, eternally abandoned. Self psychologists influenced by Winnicott prescribe empathic attunement with the "true self" as appropriate treatment. Mr. D's therapist took this approach.

> As a boy, Mr. D learned to comply with the academic and social expectations of his teachers and later reacted the same way to his employers. He eventually rose to professional success. He expected his wife and children to appreciate his efforts and recognize that he sacrificed himself for them by working so hard and being away so much. He was devastated when his wife fell in love with another man and divorced him.
>
> In therapy, he felt he could talk for the first time with someone about how unhappy and depressed he must have

been his entire life. Unable to work, he now sold what little property remained and moved to inexpensive rooms in order to support his therapy. His therapist admired his dedication to becoming adjusted to what she called the "true self." She continued to empathize with his despair until she nearly fell into her own depression. She was reluctant to recommend medication or to encourage him to become more active or more social for fear of validating "false self" functioning.

At this point, Mr. D's therapist could have outlined the predominant object relations in the therapy as in Table 2–2.

Table 2–2.   True Self-Object Relationship

Self	Affect-Sensation	Object
Depressed, true self.	Sad, empty.	Depressed mother. Absent father, wife, and children. Empathic (sad) therapist.

The relationship constellation before therapy could also be outlined as in Table 2–3.

Table 2–3.   False Self-Object Relationship

Self	Affect-Sensation	Object
Perfect, compliant, obedient self.	Superficially happy, painfree.	Admiring others.

The therapist in this example ignored her patient's adaptive ego functioning and apparently equated the adaptive ego with the false self. When the patient experienced what she called his true, depressive self-object state, he had no access to more adaptive ego capacities, which, so to speak, were in neutral or reserve, like a

computer program not booted up. Had she included ego functioning in her understanding of her patient's object relations, she might
have delineated his current predominant object relations in the
therapy as in Table 2–4.

Table 2–4. Depressed Object Relations

Self	Affect-Sensation	Object
Depressed self.	Sad, empty.	Depressed mother. Absent father, wife, and children. Empathic (sad) therapist.

Ego Functioning

Perceptions colored by sad affect. Memory selective for disappointments. Cognition limited to proving hopelessness. Actions subdued and ineffective. Modulation of self-expectation poor with an ascendence of harsh self-criticism.

The therapist changed approaches only when Mr. D needed
hospitalization because he was on the verge of suicide.

> Chatting with her patient's in-patient doctor in the hospital
> corridor, the therapist complained, "Where's his ego?"
>
> (She used the word "ego" colloquially here.)
>
> "He doesn't do anything? He just sits there, like a lump, and
> complains about being depressed? What's wrong with his
> brain?"
>
> "His brain's okay. He's just afraid to do anything competent,"
> the young doctor said, twirling a reflex hammer and teasing
> his colleague with the insolent assurance of young men who
> choose to work on psychiatric emergency wards because of
> the drama of their setting. "The moment he does something
> effective, you'll think he's a phony and won't love him any-

more." He flipped the reflex hammer into his white coat pocket like a quick-draw artist holstering his pistol, spun on his heels, and sashayed down the hall, mischievously looking at her over his shoulder.

She smiled and shook her head. "The little jerk," she said.

Until she expressed her frustration in the hospital, she had been thinking of her patient only in self-object terms and had seemed to equate her patient's adaptive ego functioning with a false self that she did not wish to engage. Using the words *self* and *ego* synonymously or discarding the ego concept entirely as impersonal or too abstract fosters such a misconception. The in-patient doctor intuitively recognized her misattribution when he teased her by saying she would consider adaptive functioning "phony."

As a child, Mr. D may have developed competence in association with a false or unreal sense of self. Equating the false self and competent ego functioning, however, seemed to interfere with the therapist's ability to help her patient engage his adaptive capacities while still genuinely unhappy. The in-patient staff members, however, could help the patient with this process, and the therapist was able to collaborate.

A few days later, Mr. D told his therapist, "I'm feeling quite a lot better. I think it's the basket weaving." His amused smile seemed that of an urbane professional, an aspect of him the therapist had not previously seen. "They have many activities. I had to do something, or they were going to put me on medicine. I didn't like the idea of occupational therapy, but that young doctor isn't as tolerant as you. I chose basket weaving, because it's such a joke—typical mental hospital.

But I actually like it. It reminds me of summer camp when we wove gimp bracelets. I made some beauties. Nobody to show them to, of course."

"Would you like to show them to someone?"

He hesitated, then said, "I guess I'm afraid if I show it to anyone, it won't be mine anymore, like the only important thing will be whether they like it or not, or whether a grown man should be weaving baskets at all." He shrugged his shoulders, a bit embarrassed.

The self psychology approach, although lacking in some regards, probably helped this patient and therapist. Once the hospital staff assisted him in reengaging his adaptive functioning, both patient and therapist seemed back on track.

> *Therapist:* What's the embarrassment about?
> *Patient:* Making a basket is such a simple thing. At least it's better than sitting in my slum dwelling, staring at the wall, thinking of suicide. *(Silence, then:)* I guess I've been wallowing in self-pity. The psychiatrist says I have to get off my ass and do something. I asked him if I should change therapists, because you're so nice and don't make me do anything.
> *Therapist:* What did he say?
> *Patient:* He's more a typical psychiatrist than you might think sometimes. He asked what I think, of course. Then he asked if I like you. I said sure I like you. And he asked if I thought you understood me, and I said sure I thought you understood me; but sometimes I wallow in self-pity because you're so nice. And he said, "If you like her and feel understood by her, why would you want to change? Just watch out for the self-pity. It's a killer." He's kind of a tough guy.

To this point in the conversation, the patient had described his ability to do something constructive if small and his fear that if someone understood the vulnerable aspects of himself, he would become dysfunctional—"wallow in self-pity." Because the therapist, at this point, had begun to think of her patient's competence as distinct from his "false self," she could now see it as integrated with his image of himself as hurt and vulnerable. She next made an integrative interpretation.

> *Therapist:* I wonder if sometimes you don't hide how bright and competent you can be for fear that I'll overlook how hurt and alone you also feel?
> *Patient:* Yeah. That, and I'm just tired of being competent. I'm pissed off, and I'm hurt, and sometimes I don't give a damn. But I did enjoy weaving the basket.

When the hospital doctor, with the therapist's concurrence, induced the patient's latent ego abilities by requiring him to do something constructive, the experience also seemed to activate his self-images of competence. The therapist helped him take an integrative step by recognizing that seeing himself as hurt and sad and as competent and active could coexist. This integration forms a new object relationship available to Mr. D (Table 2–5).

Table 2–5.   Integrated Object Relations

Self	Affect-Sensation	Object Image
Coping and able to prevail despite weaknesses.	Angry and hurt, yet determined— moderate muscle tension.	Both encouraging and understanding.

Ego Functioning

Perceptions keen. Memories well rounded. Cognition active, integrative, and humorous. Emotions mixed and modulated. Actions beginning to be constructive. Modulation of self-expectation fine-tuned.

This ability to feel hurt, yet function competently, was a new object relations style for Mr. D. Once his therapist started seeing his competence as part of him and still knew he felt sad and vulnerable in some ways, he saw himself and the people around him in a new way. He was not a sad, depressed, quiet little boy drearily communing with his depressed mother and abandoned by his father. Neither was he only the competent student, athlete, and worker his boarding school teachers and later his employers and even his wife and children had known. He was a potentially competent man whose only available coping skills had failed him, leading to a serious illness. And he had a therapist who could recognize that weaving a basket was just a start, but was confident that he could continue succeeding. Unlike his early life experience with a hypercompetent father who denied feelings and a decompensated mother overcome by emotion, his therapist and his ward doctor, as different as they were, could share insights and work together for his benefit. This teamwork, too, constituted a new external object relationship, which he could internalize and eventually make a part of himself (Gabbard 1989).

THE EGO AND SELF-HELP COUNSELING

Ego concepts can serve well in general psychiatry as well as formal psychotherapy. All doctor–patient interactions have supportive psychotherapy aspects.

A psychiatrist at the Menninger Clinic, who had been influenced by Adolph Meyer's pragmatic approaches to mental illness as well as by dynamic and biological approaches, routinely discussed with patients the risks, benefits, and alternatives to psychotherapy, medication, and self-help in regard to depression. He often gave a 2- or 3-minute psychoeducational description of a self-help approach to treating depression.

"Depression has been around long before medication or even formal psychotherapy," he would say. "In the eighteenth and nineteenth centuries, some people wrote books about how they recovered from depression. What they thought helped them were keeping a regular schedule, eating small meals at mealtime even if they weren't hungry, going to bed and getting up at the same time even if they couldn't sleep very well, exercising daily if only a walk around the yard, and working even if they couldn't concentrate very well. Prayer, formal involvement in religion, superficial social contacts, artistic endeavors, and helping others have all been beneficial to some people. We don't know how helping others helps ourselves, but there are good studies showing it does."

After some discussion, he would add, "I realize these are all things you don't feel like doing when you're depressed. I'm not saying you have to do them. What I'm saying is that if you can make yourself do some of these things, it will help, along with whatever treatment we end up using."

From the object relations viewpoint, such a behavioral and psychoeducational approach can stimulate adaptive ego functioning. This approach starkly contrasts with self psychology, which might consider encouragement as unempathic and invalidating of the cohesive self. By not demanding compliance, however, and by understanding how difficult a person who is depressed might find these activities, the psychiatrist empathically recognized his patients' debilitated self-experience and discouraged affect, while establishing himself as a helpful and considerate person who does not consider his patients helpless. Along with encouraging adaptive functioning, this collaborative approach offers patients an opportunity to experience the self as competent and effective. The drawback, of course, is that the experience could be reminiscent of a teacher–pupil or parent–child relationship, which may or may not have helpful connotations for a particular patient.

CONCLUSION

Seeing a patient as reduced to an impersonal collection of habit formations, to a mechanistic configuration of drives, defenses, and ego mechanisms, or to a system of biological feedback loops can harm the patient's self-experience of being valuable, valued, and unique. On the other hand, considering a patient solely a subjective self in relation to an empathizing object can also cause harm by denying the patient's complexity, variability over time, ability to overcome difficulty, and cognitive-perceptual-motor strengths and weaknesses. What is needed, I believe, is an integrated yet diverse and differentiated way of thinking and feeling about patients, a way that both personalizes and objectifies the work and the relationship with them.

Any theory must draw upon impersonal abstractions to some extent. The theoretical construct of self, affect-sensation, object, and ego functioning that form organically related states of mind or ways of being in relationship must also use such distancing terms. The theory's advantage, however, is its personal nature that does not sacrifice the possibility of assessing ego functioning and even of describing self-object relationships from both emotionally near and distant viewpoints (Hamilton et al. 1994). It gives the therapist the possibility of addressing issues outside the patient's current subjective feelings without necessarily damaging their integrity. While preserving the personal relationship emphasis of British object relations approaches and the intersubjectivity of self psychology

(Stolorow et al. 1992), the theory presented here reintroduces the possibility of discussing ego functions so as to acknowledge the mind–body connections Hartmann (1964), among others, postulated. The notion of affect-sensations provides another such mind–body connection that can replace focusing on drives.

The alternative, using no theory at all, although appealing to many talented therapists' intuitive nature, often results in confusion and collapses when complex cases and powerful countertransference require clear thinking about patients, therapists, and therapists in relation to their patients. Theories about people are organized, complex ways of seeing people. And how a therapist regards patients influences them powerfully for good or ill. Those who make a living helping people must give considerable thought to how their notions affect patients. A theory that proves adaptable enough to describe individuals as individuals and complex enough to treat them fairly and to surprise therapists with new insights is extremely useful for examining how therapists think about, feel toward, and relate to their patients.

3

Relationship Patterns

Kernberg (1975), Masterson (1976), and Rinsley (1978) describe all-good, all-bad split mental states in borderline patients. Shifts in mental states or relationship patterns do not occur only among people with borderline disorders. Myriad combinations and permutations of self, affect-sensation, object, and ego functioning can develop in all people, depending upon their individual characteristics and experiences.

Some common patterns of object relations include the fragmented-fused of psychotic patients, the split of borderline patients, the idealized-devalued of narcissistic individuals, the traumatized-traumatizing or victim-victimizer of trauma victims, the true versus false of schizoid and some obsessive patients, and the fairly well integrated-differentiated of healthier individuals. Upon closer examination, each person displays his or her own unique relationships. From somewhat different viewpoints, Horowitz (1979, 1991, 1992) flexibly describes states of mind and person schemas, and Stern (1985) delineates "representations of interactions that have been generalized" (p. 97). Here too the object relations approach can be used as flexibly as the clinical situation demands.

SPLITTING AND SPLIT OBJECT RELATIONS

Splitting is the mental and sometimes interpersonal activity of keeping contradictory experiences separate. Building on Klein's (1946) original definition and Fairbairn's (1954) description of divided ego–object constellations, U.S. psychiatrists consider excessive splitting a salient borderline characteristic (Gabbard 1994, Kernberg 1975), although it occurs among all people to some extent. Splitting corresponds to shifting all-good and all-bad vacillations of rapprochement-substage children in Mahler's (Mahler et al. 1975) separation–individuation schema, which describes developing object relations. Kohut (1971) and Stern (1985) consider such self-divisions breakdown products of inadequate self-object function that lead to loss of cohesion. Regardless of how authors perceive developmental ordering of splitting, however, clinicians can readily observe it. Splitting among adults is discussed here without relying on a particular theory of early development.

> When she first called a psychotherapist, Ms. E, a 32-year-old teacher, stated she had borderline "personality disorder" and needed to work with someone experienced in that area. In early sessions, she succinctly delineated her diagnostic features, which she had read about in a school manual. Forthrightly and in a calm, orderly fashion, she described herself as chaotic, impulsive, intolerant of being alone, and inclined to form intense, unstable relationships. She repeatedly fell in love with men whom she at first considered wonderful but later found terrible.

In early sessions, she spoke to the therapist as if he were a peer who was consulting with her about a student. She reminded him that she had idealized her previous therapist, then felt severely disappointed in him. She warned the new therapist that the same thing might happen with him; they would need to deal with that possibility, she suggested. Despite her clear thinking, she seemed highly anxious.

Like Chapter 1's Ms. B, this patient did not split her internal world at the moment, but displayed whole object relations. In a balanced way, she considered both an all-good self-object experience and an all-bad self-object experience with her parents, boyfriends, and former therapist. Her ego functioning seemed intact. She could cognitively hold emotional opposites in mind simultaneously while discussing past and future. As with Ms. B, however, her anxiety and intent scrutiny of the therapist indicated impaired ego functioning, even during optimal relatedness. She could not successfully modulate anxiety, and her emotional balance seemed precarious.

Her insisting on talking with her therapist like a peer rather than a patient was perhaps related to a fear of becoming dependent. Her anxiety may have arisen because, when she did feel dependent on another person, her associated affects and sensations could erupt, overwhelming her ego functioning. Evidence for this conjecture remained subtle and unconfirmed.

From earliest memory, she felt her father hated and abused her. He gave her chores above her ability, berated her when she could not accomplish them to his satisfaction, spanked her often and excessively, and doted on and favored her older sister. Her mother did not come to the rescue and seemed indifferent to her daughter's difficult situation with her father.

The patient remembered both mother and father arguing about the fact, which her mother defiantly acknowledged, that her conception had resulted from an affair with another man. Instead of being shocked, as a 5-year-old child she had felt joy and hopefulness about having a different father. "That explained it," she said. "He wasn't really my father. My real father was a good man, who would've loved and protected me. I thought about him every day of my life and vowed I'd find him when I grew up."

She felt sacrificed by her mother to her father and came to believe that her mother's refusal to help and protect her sprang from the desire to avoid her husband's jealous anger and to continue her drinking and affairs.

Although she did not feel all-good or all-bad during the session, she described past split object relations. She had often felt like a worthless, discarded, and sacrificed person in relation to uncaring or hating parents. In secret, however, she had also felt like a wonderful and valued little girl in relation to a good and rescuing fantasy-father, her "real" father. In memory, she displayed little emotional integration of these two split relationship constellations. Splitting did not manifest itself in the here-and-now therapy, however, and she still described both sides of the split with balance.

Two months later, she revealed that in adolescence, when she had learned her mother continued to see her biological father clandestinely, hope leaped up in her heart. She wanted to meet him, certain he would help her if he knew how her parents treated her. She confronted her mother, insisting she introduce her to her "real" father. In response, her mother broke off her relationship and refused to give her daughter his name or any information about him.

When the therapist asked about her feelings or empathized as she told her story, her anxiety escalated. She fended him off with cognitive understanding. "So you can see how split my world was. I need you to help me bring it together," she demanded.

Her deeper psychological world indeed seemed split. An intellectualized integration stretched thinly across inner polarities. She seemed so reasonable, however, the therapist still could not determine whether she was an obsessive, depressed, or anxiety-disordered person whose low self-esteem and guilt led her to describe herself as more disturbed than she really was. She depicted her internal world as if revealing both sides of a balance sheet to a financial adviser.

She would soon demonstrate that what she worried about and feared was that her precariously balanced whole object relations would degenerate into a split between heaven and hell, with severely compromised ego functioning at the very moment she felt strong personal emotion.

After several sessions, the therapist said, "You seem anxious. Perhaps you want me to understand you and listen to you, but the possibility also makes you nervous." He considered this a gentle, empathic comment alluding to her anxiety about openness or closeness. He feared that if he said little she would feel neglected and abandoned.

"What do you expect!" she flared. "What do you want me to do, tear open my chest and let you see my insides?"

Momentarily shocked, the therapist paused, then recovered. "Not at all," he said. "I think we should proceed slowly. Of course you would get anxious if you feel I might ask you to tear yourself open."

The alternative of proceeding slowly, however, did not present itself again for a long time. Whenever the patient discussed personal feelings, she fell into a maelstrom. The therapist would help her reorganize herself by session's end, hoping her daily duties and school structure would sustain her until the next session.

She began leaving messages on his answering machine, berating him for lack of understanding. During these tirades, her thought processes deteriorated. She confused pronouns, using "you," "I," and "them" chaotically. On occasion she produced clang associations, which give more importance to the sound of words than to their meaning, such as, "You think I'm afraid of being near, Dear. I nearly hit a deer on the road last night, but hit the brakes instead."

She no longer remembered split relationships, she experienced them. She felt attacked and fragmented; her therapist seemed threatening and unhelpful; her primary affects were anger and outrage; and her ego functioning deteriorated. For brief periods, she lost her ability to differentiate self-object images, seeing herself and her primary objects as equally and mutually destructive. Her lack of ego capacity became so pervasive she could not distinguish appropriate pronouns or similar-sounding words with different meanings. Her associations had personal meanings, but the therapist needed to sort them out because she was unable to do so.

The threat of being close to someone emotionally, of feeling even a little understood, seemed so great she might have felt like a deer on the road about to be crushed by an impersonal machine. It was not clear, however, whether the deer represented herself or her therapist, as well as a presumably actual animal she may have encountered. In the transference and her identification with the therapist, did her slamming on the brakes represent the therapist's attempt to slow down the therapy, her attempt to keep herself or the therapist intact, or something entirely different? Her self-object aspects collapsed, but her perceptions remained intact: she did not develop hallucinations or other distortions. Neither did she display fixed delusions nor lose her capacity to perform daily activities in structured situations.

At the session after her message about the deer, she described how desperate she had felt when she learned that her mother had sent away her biological father. Coherently and with considerable emotion, she told how she had then got drunk with some other high school students at a party. Driving back from the party late at night, she purposely accelerated on a tortuous mountain road until she lost control of her mother's car and crashed into a huge fir tree. She learned upon awakening in an intensive care unit that the steering wheel had torn open her chest.

"Thank God you were able to put the brakes on this time," the therapist said spontaneously.

She seemed relieved and calmed. "Yes," she said, "thank God."

In this example, split-off all-bad object relations erupted the first time she allowed herself to have strong feelings about the therapist. Did this feeling pertain to her relationship with her parents as well as her car trauma? Did it have something to do with memories of childhood beatings? Had she always reacted so strongly to emotional closeness from earliest infancy? Was her current poor emotional modulation of relationships the result of brain injury received in the car accident? The cause of the splitting remained unclear at this point. Evidence for its existence, however, was no longer just in her memories and intellectualized description. It now manifested itself in the therapy.

When her doctor spontaneously uttered, "Thank God you were able to put the brakes on this time," she seemed to realize he felt concerned about her. She could see his relief that she had not repeated her previous disaster, and she suddenly shifted to an idealized, all-good object relationship with equally lethal possibilities.

Moments later, she declared she felt loved and cared about by her therapist. In subsequent sessions, she basked in these feelings. Between sessions, she could not tolerate her loneliness and longing. She began frequenting trendy nightspots. She not only agreed to go home with the first man she met, she fawned on and idolized him. She seemed to pick such men at random. Some of them acted pleasantly enough; others did not.

One night she met a man who had no visible means of support, carried a weapon and a beeper, groomed himself menacingly, and made poor eye contact. These unsavory qualities did not register with her. She felt in blissful union with him, would do anything he asked, and turned her will completely over to him. "It could have been a disaster," she said. "Maybe he was a drug dealer. I could have been arrested and lost my job, my career. Or I could have been shot! But I didn't give it a thought until the next morning. Then I thought, 'What have I done?' "

Therapist and patient sorted out the events at the next session and noted that she did not appear to unconsciously, masochistically seek a destructive relationship. She seemed to act out her longing and found the first available man as a substitute when her therapist was not there. She would have been equally happy, she said, with a well-groomed and well-mannered businessman in town for a convention. She had just happened to run into the unsavory character.

"It was like an illusion, like this creep was Prince Charming or my real father or something. It was like this guy was a cloud on a summer day and I saw in him whatever I wanted."

She described an all-good split self–other state and actually manifested it in the treatment. Her self-image became perfect and loved, her affects loving with pleasurable and erotic sensations, her objects perfect, loving men (imagined father-therapist-lover), and her ego functioning impaired with an inability to remember con- tradictory experience, a preference for fantasy over perception, poor modulation of emotions, and impulsive action. This all-good object relationship combined with the all-bad object relations of the previous few sessions illustrates classic splitting.

Although in the session just described she seemed to have "come to her senses" and returned to whole object integration, the possibility remained that she still resided in a fantasy, all-good self–other state, this time with the therapist. She did not bring together the good and not-so-good aspects of the previous evening, but now saw them as all-bad. The therapeutic task proved compli- cated because the external reality of the previous night's events might indeed have been disastrous. Nevertheless, a fairy-tale qual- ity dominated her description. In her mind, Prince Charming had turned into a malignant and dangerous drug dealer. Any therapist would have been tempted to agree with the patient's current assessment and collude with the notion that in contrast to the dangerous city nightlife, the therapy was good and safe, almost perfect, and that the therapist was now Prince Charming or a fairy godmother who had rescued her. But the therapist had no actual evidence about what had happened the previous evening. The tendency to elicit from others affects and even perceptions corre- sponding to the patient's current internal world typifies split object relations. This interpersonal splitting is thought to be carried out via projective identification (Gabbard 1989, Hamilton 1994), often defined as the attribution of aspects of the self to another person and simultaneous reidentification with the disavowed aspects in the other.

Fortunately the patient retained integrated and whole object relatedness at times. This residual capacity suggested she had congenitally good ego functions and provided evidence that her lapses in integrative function were not caused by brain injury from the car accident. Her schooling and her relationships with teachers may have helped foster this aspect of her functioning. At any rate, the therapist elected to call upon her cognitive abilities to bring together her split experience.

"Thank goodness I'm getting help with this before it ruins my career and my future children's lives," she said.

The therapist felt less certain than she that he could help her enough soon enough to forestall further tragedy. This disparity between her hopefulness and his provided a clue that she still idealized him as an all-good object.

"You seem to be feeling a lot better about the therapy and about me than you were a few weeks ago," he said.

This statement juxtaposed the good and bad objects in the therapy (Hamilton 1988). By bringing together two split-off, emotionally powerful aspects of the therapeutic relationship, the statement served an integrative function. That is, it brought together the image of the therapist as good and understanding and the image of the therapist as intrusive, dangerous, and abandoning. His comment, however, did not have power and immediacy for the patient.

Patient: Yes. (Waits for him to go on)

Therapist: That's good. Since you've started to count on me, however, it must be at least a bit frustrating for you that I'm not there enough to protect you from these dangerous impulses.

Patient: What do you mean?

Therapist: Well, it isn't just some dangerous man who causes you trouble. You hadn't been getting involved with strangers for some months before you started therapy. But when you couldn't stand your loneliness between sessions, that's what led to your searching for someone, because I wasn't there.

Patient: Yes, but you can't be there all the time. I don't blame you. But . . . it does kind of bother me that you aren't there. You get me in touch with my feelings and then you aren't there.

The therapist carefully tried to introduce here an awareness of the ambivalence inherent in all relationships. The patient's tendency to flip-flop between all-good and all-bad relatedness, however, made it difficult and slow going.

Therapist: Yes, it's difficult for you at times.

Patient: (Snapping) So what am I supposed to do, quit therapy? That's great! Then I don't stand a chance.

She flip-flopped back to an all-bad state, as she had when she felt the therapist wanted her to tear her chest open.

Therapist: No, I think we're doing fine. I just want to look at the difficulties as well as what's fine.

Patient: (Characteristically abrupt, she shifts again) So that's the split. Either therapy is perfect or I think you are telling me to get out.

Therapist: That's the way I see it.

Patient: So what do we do about it, so I don't get in trouble between sessions?

Therapist: Let's think about that.

Ms. E was a highly intelligent and well-read woman who had undergone previous therapy. Her psychodynamic vocabulary that corresponded to some degree to the therapist's both helped and hindered their work. For the moment, she had regained whole object relatedness, with fairly good ego functioning, and could work with the therapist on a plan to forestall her desperate acting-out as treatment progressed. Nevertheless, she continued to function in split object relations for a long time. Eventually, she largely overcame this tendency.

IDEALIZED SELF, DEVALUED OTHER

The idealized self and devalued other object relations pattern arises in most individuals at one time or another and does not necessarily signify pathology. Examples from individuals with severe pathology, however, illustrate this pattern most clearly. The case of Mr. F, who had seen numerous therapists unsuccessfully, demonstrates how this style of being and relating can result in both extreme success and personal tragedy.

> Mr. F, a 46-year-old, highly influential executive, came for evaluation primarily to justify himself. He had read books about how to live with a borderline spouse. He wanted the therapist to examine his wife, confirm her personality disorder, and corroborate that all the problems in their relationship stemmed from her.
>
> A vast amount of clinical information about the couple and their children had accumulated over time. Most clinicians believed that Mrs. F probably had borderline personality disorder and might have been highly provocative toward her husband. She alternately overindulged and neglected her children. Previous marital therapists and psychotherapists had expressed different opinions about whether Mr. F was a

rigid and controlling narcissistic and obsessive individual or a man with mildly vulnerable self-esteem, trying to cope with an impossible situation at home.

As if he were running a boarding school, Mr. F attempted to structure the lives of his wife and his children, but not through personal involvement and patience. Instead he decreed the way things were to be: they were to be convenient for him so that he could devote his attention to enhancing his considerable prestige and fortune. When, in his view, his wife undermined his efforts, he sometimes flew into a rage and sometimes retreated into condescending disgust with this woman that he considered a "sick borderline."

The patient seemed to idealize himself and devalue others, rather than to split and experience self and object as either all-good or all-bad at different times.

He had been the middle son, reared in a multiply divorced and remarried family with one younger sibling, two older stepsiblings, and two younger half siblings. "As a boy," he said, "I was the problem solver and mediator. My stepdad was okay. He kind of buddied with me and we got along fine. My mom was a good mother, but she didn't have any control over the older kids, so I had to negotiate with them."

"Were they the stepkids?" the therapist asked.

"Yeah. And because she didn't have any control, we had to make deals about everything. I was a negotiator from the beginning."

"You must be proud of this ability of yours," the therapist said, attempting to recognize, perhaps empathize with, his patient's apparent affect of pride.

"Yes I am. I've never really had to work at it, though. It's just a talent I have. It's made me lots of money."

"Perhaps it was a little bit hard to have to use this skill so early, to come to terms with these complex relationships without much help. Did you ever feel a bit overwhelmed?"

"No, not really. It's never been a problem."

The therapist felt slightly rebuffed. He had tried to empathize with his patient's more vulnerable feelings while recognizing his ;trengths, but the patient was having none of it.

One cannot tell with certainty from this example alone whether the therapist's feeling of being rebuffed resulted from his own competitiveness and narcissistic vulnerability or from a reaction to the patient's subtly demeaning attitude. Very likely, the patient did indeed act so as to demean the therapist, *and* the therapist was somewhat sensitive to issues of pride and competition. Definite answers to such questions usually cannot be given, but it is often useful to ask them nonetheless. At a later session the therapist returned to this topic.

Therapist: Being so skillful a deal maker in your early life and your current work, it must disappoint you that you can't negotiate things with your wife in a way that provides more stability in your home.

Patient: I can. We negotiate things out fine and come to an agreement. Then she goes off on some wild tangent and does whatever pops into her head, even with simple things. Just last week we agreed that the kids have to have a set bedtime. She said 10. I said 9. We compromised on 9:30, no problem. Everything's fine. Then, last night, I come home from a meeting at 10:30, and they're all in bed with her, watching movies, cozy and comfy, slurping milkshakes and getting buttered popcorn all over the sheets. Suddenly, I'm the bad guy if I make 'em go to bed. It'd piss off a saint. So I said, as calmly as I could, "Come on kids. It's past your bedtime." They begged to watch the end of the show, of course. When I insisted, I raised my voice just barely, entirely appropriate. She started sobbing and clutching the kids to her. "Don't hit my babies! Don't hit my babies!" I had no intention of hitting them! And they aren't babies. They're 12 and 14. When she makes me look like some abusive stereotype, it makes me lose it. I hadn't felt like hitting anyone earlier, but I sure felt like smacking her then.

Therapist: Did you?

Patient: Of course not! This woman is sick. I mean how can you want to hit someone so pathetic?

Therapist: It's tough to believe it's despicable to even feel like hitting someone you see as so pathetic, yet to actually feel like "smacking her."

Patient: Anyone would feel that way. You're the expert. Isn't that true? Isn't that normal?

The therapist felt momentarily helpless.

Whether or not the patient's reaction was an understandable human emotion, he repeated his characteristic way of acting in relationships. He saw himself as idealized, perfectly reasonable, responsible, and normal and his wife as utterly pathetic. This self-object pattern also arose with the therapist, who had a choice either to agree with and confirm the patient's preferred view of himself and fix the impossible situation or to join the wife, in the patient's mind, as pathetic and incompetent. The patient's affect in such a self-other state was indignant. Ego functioning was directed toward annihilating opposing arguments and viewpoints and expressing his considerable rage. In that he could not consider alternative viewpoints, his ego functioning was impaired. Even empathy apparently threatened his view of himself as perfect.

"A lot of people in your situation would feel trapped and helpless," the therapist persisted. "But that feeling is difficult for you to tolerate."

"Isn't it for everyone?" the patient indignantly answered.

"Sure. Yes, I suppose it is," the therapist agreed. He felt sad and resigned. He thought Mr. F could not tolerate feeling weak, helpless, sad, or vulnerable and hypothesized that the patient had acted in such a way as to elicit those affects in him, the therapist. But he wasn't sure. Maybe he was being too blunt or impatient or hadn't found the right approach.

The patient calmed considerably when the therapist decided to tolerate his own feelings of helplessness rather than try to help the patient with his.

Mr. F seemed to attribute whatever weakness or powerlessness he might have felt to thee
the therapist and Mrs. F. He tried to control the disavowed aspects of himself that he saw in Mrs. F by criticizing and berating her or by providing guidance and structure. He behaved toward the therapist so as to elicit in him feelings of being trapped and helpless that corresponded to what he, the patient, might have felt. This process of projective identification (Gabbard 1989, Grotstein 1981, Hamilton 1988, Kernberg 1975, Klein 1946, Ogden 1982, Scharff and Scharff 1992) is the vehicle for shifting and dividing self and others in various object relations. Thus, idealization and devaluing occur not only between self and other, they can also take place between self and self and object and object. From this viewpoint, Mr. F might have had complementary, unconscious, idealized-devalued object relations in which he himself felt devalued in relation to the object. If he could not tolerate this self-experience, he might attribute it to the other through projective identification. Because the therapy failed to progress, further evidence for this hypothesis could not be gathered in this case.

Over time, Mr. F seemed so desperate to attribute devalued aspects of himself to his wife and see himself as perfect that he could neither let her go nor learn to better understand and tolerate her behavior and his reactions. He frequently threatened divorce and sometimes filed for divorce, but did not follow through on his decision. "She's so pathetic she needs me," he would say.

The patient stopped treatment, which was probably not a true therapy because Mr. F had never asked for help with his own difficulties. He said he considered the therapist a nice fellow, but perhaps the case was just too difficult for him. Five-year follow-up revealed that he and his family remained enmeshed in the same destructive relationships.

Not all idealized-self, devalued-other object relations become so entrenched. Many people fall into such a pattern only when their self-esteem is threatened in some way. Physicians commonly develop this reaction when facing difficult clinical situations.

Dr. G's colleagues referred this well-trained cardiologist for treatment because he periodically berated, then refused to see, a whole class of patients. Such behavior jeopardized the group's practice.

"This is not an issue of being an impaired physician or being required to come here," Dr. G said. "Usually I'm just fine. I'm typically a considerate and respectful professional. I get along fine with patients and colleagues both. I do well with my family too. My wife and I have our issues, but no big crisis. I get along with the kids fine. Sometimes I feel guilty for working too hard, but I take weekends off and only take calls every three weeks. Most people think I'm okay. I guess I am. But with certain kinds of patients, I lose it. I act like the biggest jerk. I get indignant, and I guess I better fix that."

"Let's hear about it," the psychiatrist said. "What kind of patients are you talking about? What happens?"

Unlike Mr. F, Dr. G knew he had a problem. He accepted that fact and contrasted it with his view of himself as a good doctor and a decent person. He did not seem especially threatened by the need to seek help and treated the psychiatrist as a competent professional.

> *Patient:* They're always the same. Alcoholic smokers with cardiomyopathy or coronary artery disease, either one, who won't quit smoking and drinking. It drives me nuts. I'm okay till they start complaining and whining and demanding I do more and more. They typically want some procedure, but they won't give up their habits that led to the problem. They won't even take the medicine I give them correctly. They won't eat properly. They won't lose weight. *(More and more indignant)* They won't exercise. All they do is criticize and hassle, because I can't fix them. But I can't! What can I do if they don't even try? *(Practically shouting)* These people disgust me!

He lost his composure. He could no longer think or feel in a balanced or modulated way. His affects overwhelmed his ego, and his overvalued self felt contempt for the objects of his wrath.

> *Therapist:* It sounds like you believe you should be able to do something about it, like you aren't a good doctor if you can't help everyone.
> *Patient: (Calming down)* Yes, I know. See how wound up I get? What do you think? Can you fix it?

Although there are other theoretical formulations for this interaction, according to the concept of shifting object relations states, Doctor G can be described as a man who usually functioned in a well-integrated and -modulated, whole self-object state. Certain individuals, however, triggered his tendency to see himself as superior and competent and others as inferior, incomprehensible, and disgusting. His affect at such times grew indignant and angry, and his ego functioning became momentarily devoid of the ability to consider alternatives, to empathize, to find creative solutions, or even to temporize. He could shift back to a more balanced perspective and relatedness rather quickly. These fluctuations seemed evident in the session, although not initially in the transference itself, except perhaps subtly, in the way he said, "Can you fix it?" as if it were a demand rather than a question.

Over the next several sessions, Dr. G revealed that he had been reared by a mother and father with problems similar to those of the patients he resented so bitterly. His mother preoccupied herself with her own hypochondriacal concerns and used a pharmacopeia of remedies, including numerous sedatives, none of which helped. She seldom paid attention to her son's interests and concerns. His father worked excessively outside the home, avoided his wife whose self-pitying monologues annoyed him, and frequently drank to the point of stuporous intoxication on weekend evenings. Six weeks into the therapy:

Patient: My mother thought our family doctor was wonderful even though nothing he did helped her very much. I went to high school with his son. I remember when I was 14 actually thinking, "I have two choices here. I can either be like my parents and go completely down the tubes or I can be like the doctor." Obviously I decided to be like the doctor. I studied. I worked my rear off to get money for college. I played football and was president of the honor society.

Therapist: It must Eave been hard doing all that on your own.

Patient: Yes, it was hard. But the choice was clear. When other kids started drinking beer, I didn't touch the stuff. I still don't. I had friends, and people liked me, but mostly I worked and followed the rules.

Therapist: And you believed you couldn't let down your guard at all. Right?

Patient: Yeah, I think I'd still be that way if it weren't for the classes they made us take in medical school about physicians' lifestyles and if I didn't have such a great wife. She's understanding, but she lays down the law when it's time for me to take some time off.

Therapist: So you even follow the rules about what is healthy when you relax and take time off?

(Up to this point the therapist was primarily paraphrasing his patient's remarks.)

Patient: (Laughing) I guess I do.

A few weeks later they returned to the same topic.

Patient: I'm afraid not to follow the rules, because if I don't. . . . (Stops)

Therapist: Are you afraid you'll turn out like your parents at their worst?

In patients with polarized object relations the inverse of the presenting self–other constellation typically is warded off, often unconscious but powerfully present. In Dr. G's case he wanted help with the idealized self and devalued object scenario, but the inverse, the passive and devalued self in relation to disparaging objects, needed to be elucidated and addressed.

Patient: Or like these patients I can't tolerate. It's funny. I tolerate my parents now. I feel sorry for them. They are old and not very healthy. I don't like to be around them a lot, but I can tolerate them. It's an obligation.

Therapist: Perhaps these patients not only represent your parents but yourself, what you feared you would become if you let down your guard, if you didn't work all evening saving money for school and study half the night.

Patient: Do you think I hate these patients, because? . . . You know, I actually feel hatred for them. I'm ashamed of that, but I do feel that way at times. Do you think I hate them because I can't stand myself?

Therapist: Perhaps because you dislike what you might have become.

Patient: And what I could still become. I still think I could be like that. They make me feel helpless. I can't afford to feel that way. I'm still afraid to touch a drop of alcohol for fear I'll start drinking and not quit. I'm afraid to take a day off when I have a cold, because I might not get up and go back to work.

Therapist: It must take courage to recognize that.

Patient: Everything has taken courage. It's been too hard for too long.

Tears showed in his eyes but did not pour forth. He had not shed a tear since, as a high school student, he had made a choice to be like the doctor he idealized. He did not actually sob now either, but dried his moist eyes and went back to work.

Gradually Dr. G came to tolerate his frustrated feelings with certain patients and no longer lost his temper. He did not cease feeling irritated at times. Although he had initially hoped to eliminate all such feelings, he instead relinquished this perfectionistic wish as unattainable and unnecessary.

In this example Dr. G's need to see himself as superior and others as inferior did not dominate his entire personality. In object relations terms, when threatened with feelings of helplessness, he feared identifying with the least functional aspects of certain patients. He must have developed a similar fear as a boy, who would naturally want to identify with his parents but at the same time feared to do so. When such feelings arose, he used projective identification to reestablish his views of himself as competent and superior and the patient as inferior and out of control. The therapy helped him to recognize and accept the helpless and help-seeking aspects of himself, rather than to project these aspects onto his patients and then try to control his own unwanted feelings in his interactions with the patients. Dr. G, unlike Mr. F, confirmed that his idealized-self, devalued-other polarity overlay an unconscious devalued self-experience that he feared.

Why do individuals like Mr. F develop pervasive narcissism and others like Dr. G display only narcissistic episodes? It is tempting to attribute the difference to constitutional, autonomous ego strength. Both Dr. G and Mr. F, however, had considerable cognitive and perceptual-motor abilities. Why did they use them in distinct ways? Perhaps the answer lay in their developmental histories. Both came from difficult backgrounds; both lacked appropriate recognition of, tolerance of, and help with their childhood weaknesses and problems. Perhaps there were subtle differences in their relationships with their neighbors, friends, teachers, coaches, and pastors. Perhaps they made different choices, existential choices so to speak, at crucial developmental stages. The deterministic dream of delineating exact causation is not fulfilled by the theory set forth in this book anymore than it is by other theories. But the theory does describe relationship patterns that may be useful to the therapist and sometimes to the patient.

VICTIM–VICTIMIZER

At first glance, the victim–victimizer relationship resembles the devalued self-idealized other, but they are in fact strikingly different. Victim–victimizer and idealized other-devalued self are neither synonyms nor antonyms. The devalued self considers the idealized object morally superior as well as more powerful and functionally effective. On the other hand, the victim self feels morally superior to, but functionally less effective and powerful than, the victimizing object.

Working with individuals who see themselves predominantly as victims and others predominantly as victimizers can be daunting. The therapist has only two readily available roles in the patient's eyes, a good but ineffective person who cannot help or a powerful person who harms the patient. The alternative of neither helping nor harming often seems cruelly neglectful and therefore victimizing to the patient, as if the powerful object were willfully withholding an ability to help. The possibility that someone might assist more than harm or might help a little does not occur to such patients. Society has compounded the therapeutic difficulties by glorifying "innocent victims" in the news, arts, courts, clinics, and schools. Therapists who agree that weakness is good and strength bad can covertly victimize the patient by overvaluing the patient role. Their solicitude can keep such patients weak.

Fortunately, some victimized individuals have other internal relationships and abilities available to them. Although many victims, possibly the majority of such patients, cannot be helped by psychotherapy, some can. The following example comes from the less common group, those who improve.

> Mrs. H, a 34-year-old teacher, had lost her husband, her health, her home, her job, and most of her friends over the past five years. She verged on losing her children. Life had been more than unfair to her.
>
> Upon graduating from college, she taught in under-developed countries. After meeting and marrying her husband, the couple worked in an impoverished section of a West Coast city. Jobs were plentiful in the inner city, they wanted to help others, and they could afford the rent while they saved money to buy a house.

With this bit of history, one can speculate that the patient had initially seen herself as a compassionate person, who could help others equally valuable but less economically fortunate. Her unconscious motivations were not apparent. Perhaps she had already identified with victims or had a reaction formation, thereby turning whatever identification with oppressors she may have had into its opposite. Nevertheless, identifying with victims and helping them, for whatever reason, demonstrates a complex and integrated self-image.

After their two children reached school age, the couple used all their savings and credit to buy a home in a suburb whose school district was excellent. As they commuted from work to their new home one evening, a drunken driver crossed the freeway median and struck their car. Mr. H died immediately. Mrs. H remained hospitalized for two months with chest and leg injuries. Complicating infections kept her wounds from completely healing for two years.

For months, friends and relatives gathered around her in support, but eventually the glamour of her tragedy wore thin. Her constant preoccupation with loss and injustice began to alienate even her closest supporters. Her increasing emotional withdrawal separated her from her few remaining loyal friends. A protracted lawsuit failed: the drunk driver, the insurance company, and other responsible parties did not have sufficient funds for a settlement. She persisted from a sense of justice, depleting her insignificant emotional and financial reserves. She felt betrayed by society and eventually by her attorney.

Unable to make house payments and caught in a temporary real estate recession, she lost her home. She was forced to move back to the inner city with her children, but feared for their safety. She had repetitive nightmares, about arsonists destroying everything around her. She feared intruders in the night. When she began missing work to protect her children during the day, she lost her job, unfairly, she believed.

Without employment, she had no medical insurance and could no longer see her counselor and her psychiatrist. At any rate, she said, treatment had not helped. Adequate trials of antidepressant and antianxiety medications only made matters worse with their side effects. Her counselor had cared about her and seemed to understand. When she persistently explored the nightmares and memories of the accident, however, they grew worse, not better. Months later, the counselor had suggested that Mrs. H might have been molested as a child and for this reason could not recover from the car accident trauma. "I got so confused I didn't know what was going on," she told her new therapist, a psychologist whose primary experience was in testing indigent patients at a public mental health clinic.

At this point Mrs. H, understandably enough, saw herself as a helpless victim of the accident, society, unfair employers, abandoning friends, nightmares, imagined intruders, medications, and misguided counselors. Other people were powerful and dangerous. Terror, despondency, and indignant, impotent rage dominated her emotions. She even felt traumatized by her own affects. Her ego functioning focused on a search for potential agents of further trauma in order to avoid them. Paradoxically, this preoccupation left her vulnerable to further victimization because she could not carry out constructive, everyday activities. Fortunately, that was not all there was to her.

Her new psychologist—young, bright, well trained—had a good heart and judgment. He had little interest in psychodynamics at this stage of his career, but understood the concepts. He preferred to work at cognitive testing and to spend off hours in athletic endeavors or socializing with other young professionals. He took an interest in Mrs. H partially because her intelligence, education, and economic background coincided with his own. In conference he told a consultant:

> *Therapist:* I feel like she fell into this mess, like she doesn't belong here. I have an impulse to rescue her. I'm not usually into rescuing people, so I hang back. I can't fight her demons for her.
> *Consultant:* So what are you doing for her?
> *Therapist:* Not much. This is a bright woman. She should be able to do something. She scored in the superior range on both the verbal and performance scales.
> *Consultant:* You tested her?
> *Therapist: (Shrugs and grins)* I didn't know what else to do, so I gave her a test.

The conference members chuckled along with the psychometrician who, under the guise of not knowing much, teased the psychoanalytic consultant.

> *Consultant:* What else did you learn from your tests?
> *Therapist:* While she was taking them, she seemed totally confident and competent. That must have been what she was like before the accident.
> *Consultant:* Did you tell her what you thought, or were you afraid it would challenge her victim role too much?
> *Therapist: (With false naïveté)* The possibility of challenging her victim role didn't cross my mind. I told her. She knew it anyway. She said she relaxes when she does tasks or games, plays fish or crazy eights with her kids, or something like that. She used to be a tournament bridge player.
> *Consultant:* This is not psychoanalysis, of course. *(Conference members chuckle)* Neutrality would be too abandoning for her, and

she might see it as further victimization. In her previous therapy, empathy with her despair only led to more despair. With this kind of patient you might want to find her strengths, the vestiges of her positive self-regard, so you have something to build on. For instance, you might encourage her to join a bridge club, so she can win at something and have something other than trauma and loss in her life. What did you do?

Therapist: I encouraged her to join a bridge club. (*More chuckles from the audience*)

Consultant: Did she?

Therapist: No. She brought a deck of cards. I played gin with her, but unfortunately I won. (*More laughter*)

Perhaps the joking and laughter derived from the therapist's own callous denial of his helplessness and victimization, like Dr. G's reaction. Perhaps the therapist's denial arose from a reaction against his identification with an oppressor or a view of the consultant as oppressive. Perhaps it was primarily legitimate professional rivalry. Such speculations remain unclear.

Therapist: I'm sorry. I guess I'm playing around too much. I really don't quite know what I'm doing and would like some help.

Consultant: On the contrary, you seem to know exactly what you're doing. Do you expect you will be able to help her?

Therapist: The way I see it, this is a competent woman whose overwhelming tragedies have led to so much affect it interferes with her ability to think. In your system, as I understand it, her affects cloud her ego functioning. She gets caught in a bottomless pit of despair and can't remember that she has ever been competent or that she can be again. When she has an affect-neutral task, she does fine, so I'm trying to provide affect-neutral tasks.

I have a cognitive and educational psychology background and can handle that part of it. What I'm afraid of is that when I get to the point of not only helping her recall her strengths but of expecting her to build upon them, she might feel I'm insensitive to expect her to get on with her life after all these losses. It's all that dynamic stuff I'm not sure about.

Consultant: Since this is supportive treatment, when the time comes, you might want to share your concern with her. Tell her you're afraid she'll think it insensitive of you to expect her to use her strengths to get on with life. If you want to be technically correct and don't want to talk about your own concerns or fears, you could ask if she thinks it would be insensitive of her to get on with things.

Therapist: No, I'd just as soon not be technically correct.

Consultant: That's obvious!

From the object relations viewpoint, the psychologist presented the case of a highly competent woman, who had been traumatized, as he noted, to the point where her affects overwhelmed her ego functioning and her earlier successful, safe, and loving self–other experiences. While he used some behavioral and cognitive restructuring to help her focus on and utilize her assets, he raised the issue of insensitivity. Would it somehow dishonor the memory of what and whom she had lost if she forgot, set the past aside, and went on with life? In the countertransference reflected in the conference, issues of insensitivity, vulnerability, dominance, and competition revealed themselves in repartee. What pertained to the conference members and what to the patient remained uncertain.

At conference six months later, the consultant asked the psychologist how Mrs. H was doing.

"She's making progress," he said. "She's in a bridge club and is substitute-teaching. She hasn't mentioned fears of her house being broken into for several months. She's even gone out to dinner with a man once."

"To what do you attribute your success?" the consultant asked, thinking he was setting up another joke and expecting the psychologist to say something along the lines of "Cognitive and behavioral therapy takes the day," or to affect naïveté by saying, "I have no idea." But the psychologist wasn't joking today.

Perhaps with some success, the therapist felt less overstimulated by the patient's victimization and had less need to rise above it with humor—humor with an edge to it.

Therapist: The cognitive and behavioral tasks may have helped. They gave her a chance to feel competent and use her good mind again. As you would say, they drew her out of her traumatized self–affect–object–ego state. When we talked about my expectation that she improve, however, she surprised me. She thought for a moment and said, "No, that's what my husband would have wanted. He would have wanted me to go on, for the children's sake and for my own sake. I guess I have to get on with things."

Consultant: What did you say?

Therapist: Something simple and cognitive like, "And you do that by returning your attention to the task at hand, like turning a switch, by not thinking about the loss for a little while and going on with what you need to do." She can do that. She's a brave lady. She says she's doing it for her children, but I think she's also doing it for the memory of her husband and for herself, maybe even for me a bit too. But we can't entirely get rid of the nightmares. She still has them every few weeks. Do you have any ideas about that?

Consultant: Not really. She may be stuck with them periodically. We can't undo the events that have happened.

Therapist: What do you mean?

A series of complex formulations leaped to the consultant's mind. They seemed too abstract. Instead, he spoke simply.

Consultant: When things this bad happen to people, it changes them forever. We can't erase the past, so it can always return to them in their memories and nightmares, at least from time to time. You're doing a fine bit of work. Just keep at it, until she decides she doesn't need you anymore.

What helped Mrs. G? Perhaps enough time had passed for her to go on with her life. Perhaps the cognitive-behavioral interventions alone helped. Perhaps losing her job and feeling the need to care for her children forced her to recognize that she must cope better. Perhaps her therapist reminded her of her husband, who would have cared about her loss, but would have wanted her to go on. Perhaps the therapist's playful false modesty and underlying self-confidence offered her an alternative to a more extreme victim–victimizer relatedness in which she had seemed trapped.

The single most important factor that helped her, however, probably resided within her. Despite the victimized self-object state described above, other self-object experiences, affects, and ego functioning remained available to her as potentials. Her psychologist reminded her of these potentials. According to the viewpoint presented in this book, she could shift back to a previously available and more adaptive way of being and relating.

FALSE SELF, TRUE SELF

Winnicott's (1965) description of false-self functioning appeals at various times to many authorities. As mentioned in Chapter 2, he ascribed false-self functioning to an early childhood characterized by parenting not good enough (1968) for the infant's needs. Children's superficial compliance with parental expectations may predominate over their true needs when they first establish a fundamental sense of self in relation to others. Parental denial of or inability to recognize a child's true affects and needs can become so compelling that the child's only way to maintain closeness is to identify with and actually experience the self as if the self *were* the parental expectations. This reaction can lead to a feeling of not being quite real, of nothing being quite real. Winnicott suggested that the result is a concomitant, deeply unconscious, and secret sense that the false self hides and protects the "true," vulnerable, lonely, and outraged self.

This relationship constellation differs from previously described ones in that 'it emphasizes the self–self rather than the self–other relationship. In false-self functioning, no true self-object distinction exists. Everything becomes self, even the object's expectations. Nothing seems quite real because a person must have a self-object duality to define real versus not real (Hamilton 1988, Modell 1968). Even superficial relatedness and social gregariousness become illusory in false-self functioning. They overlie and obscure a more fundamental withdrawal from the external world, akin to the schizoid alienation and withdrawal described by Fairbairn (1954) and Guntrip (1969).

Such a personal style, denoting deep-seated and severe pathology, can be found among highly adaptive and successful individuals. These people feel their lives are somehow empty and meaningless despite their apparent success. Histrionic characters, who identify with the wishes and expectations of the person or persons at hand, can be "false." Alternatively, false-self functioning can accompany obsessive character, in which individuals identify with the task at hand and preoccupy themselves with a highly intellectual internal world in an abstract, removed way.

Such individuals present serious treatment difficulties fraught with paradox. The therapy, like other relationships, seems not quite real to such patients. They may conform to the therapist's expectations up to a point but without genuine relatedness. They may adapt to any theoretical system yet not actually improve, as Mr. D's example shows.

Mr. D, the attorney described in Chapter 2, lost his family, career, and mental health. He had functioned competently until his wife left him on the grounds that he was never emotionally there for her or anyone else. She accurately if unsympathetically claimed he didn't even know who he was or what he wanted, or what went on with her and the children. When he looked inside himself in his therapy, he found nothingness and confusion.

In a way, his wife might have been both correct and incorrect. Such patients actually often perceive others quite sensitively, yet as if they themselves, not the people around them, were not quite real.

He intuitively knew what his employers expected from him and conformed with those expectations as if they were his own. When his therapist silently agreed with his ex-wife's opinion that he was shallow and emotionally empty, with largely false adaptive functioning, he automatically complied with her implied expectation that he should give up his traditional trappings of success and look inward. What he found was emptiness and despair, as the therapist had suspected.

Such patients are so compliant that therapists often cannot tell whether the emptiness inside represents the patients' true, subjective self-experience or their unconscious awareness that the therapist had anticipated finding emptiness.

Mr. D became an outstanding and dedicated patient, but he grew increasingly impaired and eventually suicidal.

The patient apparently had not dropped his false-self stance but had adopted another one, this time identified with the therapist's inclination that he should exclusively attend to his sad feelings.

One paradox of the false self, however, is that what is false may also be true. This factor became obvious in the example of Mr. D discussed in Chapter 2, when the in-patient doctor reminded the therapist of the validity and usefulness of the patient's compliant ego functioning.

> Mr. D became marginally more functional and less despon-dent after the hospitalization when he and his therapist recognized that she could value his competence and his pain and loss simultaneously. He by no means recovered, however. For several months he remained vaguely superficial in his partial improvement, as if he now identified with her more integrated view of competent behavior in the face of sadness and loss.
>
> The therapist began to feel mocked by this appearance of recovery. She hesitated to suggest he might be angry for fear that she might suggest another affect with which he could identify. "Do you ever get frustrated with me because your progress has slowed?"
>
> "That's kind of a subtle slam," he said with detached amusement.
>
> "I suppose it is, in a way," she said. "Could you tell me more precisely how you see it as a 'slam'?"

She carefully tried to learn about him so he could experience himself more genuinely. To do that, the therapist did not deny her own reality as a separate, external person whom the patient may correctly perceive (Winnicott 1949).

> "So you think I'm progressing slowly? What do you expect of me? Sometimes I think you understand, and sometimes I

think you're just another woman who doesn't know what she wants from me."

This seemed like genuine affect and a real relationship, or at least a true transference; it had immediacy and intensity. The patient's search for his genuine feelings in an expensive therapy while he starved, alone in a shabby apartment, may have been a mockery of his ex-wife's and his therapist's demand that he be more "genuine," more emotionally attuned, and less task and success oriented. The slow progress in therapy may have reflected his frustrated feelings. Now his verbal expression of annoyance and his questioning of the other's expectations seemed the beginning of differentiating self and other.

> *Therapist:* No wonder you're angry.
> *Patient:* (Angrily) Who said I was angry?
> *Therapist:* (Flatly) Perhaps I'm putting words in your mouth. Perhaps you weren't angry when I first suggested the possibility. But you sound pretty annoyed right now. Are you annoyed, or do you just sound that way? Which is it?
> *Patient:* Right now I feel trapped.

His argumentativeness did not seem like the enmeshed closeness sometimes found in arguing, but suggested that he did see himself as separate from the object's, his therapist's, expectation.

> *Therapist:* (Sitting back in her chair and relaxing) I don't mean to trap you. (Appearing to wait, not knowing what to do or what would happen next)
> *Patient:* So now you aren't going to help at all!

In Winnicott's interpretation this outburst may have represented a transferential repetition of feeling emotionally abandoned, an eruption of the abandoned and outraged "true self."

Therapist: I'm listening.

Patient: I'm not used to feeling this out of control. I'm afraid if I don't tell you I'm angry, I won't be a good patient, and you'll give up on me. And if I do tell you I'm angry, then you'll think I'm just another angry man and kick me out.

If the therapist's goal had been to uncover unconscious anger as a drive derivative defended against, she might have felt thwarted by his slipping away from the issue of anger and discussing feeling trapped instead. The therapist, however, wanted to give him the opportunity to define himself in relation to another person, as he was when he felt trapped by her.

The therapist could have gone on to remind him that he had also felt trapped by his wife and could have suggested that his parents had put him in a similar situation. The only way he could be with them was to be no one at all, caught in the trap set by his parents. To make a fuller transference interpretation, however, might have suggested to him that his true feelings about her, the therapist, were not quite real, but were somehow an illusory recapitulation.

Fortunately she could let him discover who he was in relation to her, beginning with the less pleasant aspects of the relationship. *Discover* may not be the best word: more specifically, he developed or created a new sense of self in relation to another, a sense of self he had never previously experienced.

CONCLUSION

Predominant and secondary senses of self in relation to others, affects, and functional and potentially available ego abilities are useful for describing any patient. Each person's internal and external relationships differ from another's, although certain common themes, such as those described above, are apparent. Looking at general themes can be useful for broadening clinical experience and thinking through issues, but reducing an individual to a formula can be diminishing in itself by devaluing a person's ability to grow and change in unexpected ways. Therapists must consider the ways their own thinking and attitudes may affect the patient and her or his sense of relatedness in the therapy.

Therapists can easily delineate a patient's primary object relations patterns superficially. As the patient's story unfolds— history, background, current troubles and successes—as therapists observe how the patient tells the story, interacts with them, affects them, and is affected by them, they can begin to list the self-images, object images, and corresponding affects and ego functioning even in healthier individuals. The story becomes clear soon enough, the theme apparent, without reducing it to a formula plot.

This approach to object relations allows the clinician to describe each individual individually, to delineate and name internal and external relationships specifically. Yet to meaningfully understand a patient, therapists must accept that however necessary a systematic approach may be, no system does the individual justice, no understanding is ever complete. To give patients room to grow and change, therapists must acknowledge that future events are not entirely predictable.

4

Object Relations among Healthier Individuals

Having found object relations concepts useful with borderline patients, I began thinking in terms of these ideaa when treating healthier individuals (Hamilton 1992b, Hamilton et al. 1994). Although my approach here derives from and builds on many of Kernberg's ideas, it stands in contrast to his clear differentiation between models for understanding borderline and healthier individuals (Hamilton 1992b, Kernberg 1975, 1992). Kernberg shifts from an object relations viewpoint for psychotic and borderline disorders to an ego psychology, structural viewpoint for neurotic disorders. He seems to consider object relations theory central for dealing with the former and id, ego, and superego theory central for treating the latter.

In practice, distinguishing the best way to understand and treat neurotic and borderline, pre- and postoedipal, pre- and post-structuralization problems remains difficult. Most therapists familiar with ego psychology and object relations theory use aspects of both to describe all patients at different times. Healthier individuals probably have residual primitive functioning, which clinicians discuss using object relations terminology; more disorganized patients can be considered to have incompletely developed, but nevertheless present, id, ego, and superego structures, which clinicians describe using those terms. Alternatively, since all individuals have relationships, this theory may apply to healthier people as well; but an object relations model of healthier psychological functioning has not yet been used systematically. Lacking familiarity with object relations understanding of neurotic difficulties, clinicians may shift viewpoints unnecessarily and be thrown back on a structural concept that contains and builds on a no longer useful nineteenth-century notion of drives.

Over the past several years, after having added ego functioning to object relations theory, I have used this revised viewpoint alone for both healthier and more disorganized patients, to learn whether it provides an adequately flexible model for a diverse population. Chapter 4 discusses two examples of object relations theory applied to healthier individuals, using relationship patterns as the primary structural concept, without invoking tripartite theory or analyzing defense against drive or superego pressures. Differences, of course, can be found between borderline and normal or neurotic personalities, but these differences are here considered in terms of integration and differentiation within object relations, including ego function, without shifting to id, ego, and superego concepts.

Clinical vignettes about healthier individuals can be more complex than some of the stereotyped patterns described in Chapter 3: the patients have flexible, variable, and integrated patterns of thinking, being, and relating.

DEPRESSED OBJECT RELATIONS

Mrs. I, a 41-year-old homemaker, came to treatment with several weeks' history of crying, insomnia, sadness, irrita-

bility, low self-esteem, disinterest in sex, and general lassi-
tude. She said that dissatisfaction with her life at home
bothered her most.

"I'm becoming a 'dissatisfied housewife,'" she complained. "How typical! You probably see this all the time. I
don't want to be just another angry woman complaining
about her lot in life. I have a good life. I have a great husband,
good kids, a beautiful house, and lots of friends. I'm on the
board of the art museum and president of the parent-teacher
association. I've always enjoyed these activities. I'm busy but
take pride in what I do. Some classmates from college, who
have very successful careers, wish they could trade places with
me. But now nothing seems right. I don't even like myself. If I
keep this up, Dan won't like me either. How could he?"

Focusing on her marriage, the therapist asked, "How are
you and your husband doing?"

She explained that since she had become depressed, he
spent time talking with her into the night after the children
were in bed. He was supportive, willing to adjust their lifestyle, interested, and tolerant. He showed concern but not
excessive worry. "Sure, he gets annoyed at times, but not
often. Being around a depressed person can be a pain. I don't
know how he stands me," she said.

"It sounds like you're less tolerant of your own dissatisfaction right now than anyone else is," the therapist said. He
also wondered if she might be seeing her housewife role and
her husband in an idealized manner, perhaps defensively, but
he thought it unwise to address that in an initial session.

For the moment, the therapist took the patient's description
of herself and her husband at face value. Using this work's object
relations approach, the clinician may consider a relationship

description valid. Reaction formation, asserting the opposite of an emotional reality, is a defense against losing a valued relationship. In this case, Mrs. I may have defended against acknowledging conflicting aspects of her role and her relationship with her husband by idealizing him and devaluing herself, thereby protecting a cherished and idealized internal relationship. If it is later found that the idealization defends against a warded-off, unhappy relationship, both object relations patterns remain valid psychological realities.

> The therapist continued, "You even seem a bit concerned I won't take you seriously if you complain, that I'll see you as a stereotyped 'dissatisfied housewife.' "
>
> "I know. It's just me. My kids are even putting up with me."

Mrs. I, disparaging herself, revealed a transference expectation that her psychiatrist would not take her seriously if she complained. She saw herself as a "dissatisfied housewife," whose complaints had credence neither in her own eyes nor in those of her doctor, whom she suspected would see her as a "typical case." Actually the psychiatrist did not deem her weak or unnecessarily complaining. Her referring internist had said she was a "sophisticated and accomplished" woman, who had been healthy all her life and who was suffering a first episode of depression. The psychiatrist expected her to complain about her depression. Notably, she revealed a worry that her husband would lose interest in her if she complained, just as she expected the psychiatrist to do, although she also presented evidence to the contrary with her husband. Her here-and-now transference coincided with her feelings about her husband. A consistency in relatedness, a relationship pattern, had already manifested itself.

In object relations terms Mrs. I exhibited a depressed state. She felt devalued by a disparaging yet idealized object and generated affects of guilt, shame, and dissatisfaction. Her ability to remember she had felt better, to still take pride in herself, and to have hopes for the future distinguished her depressed mental state from the despondent, all-bad object relations that borderline patients often display. She could recall positive aspects of her life, although they contrasted with her current feelings. This good ego functioning, evidenced by integration of nuanced emotional crosscurrents, is typical of neurotic as opposed to borderline disorders.

In the opening minutes of the first session, information about Mrs. I's internal relationships already presented itself. With an object relations approach, a first tentative formulation is immediately available in transference and countertransference without a high degree of abstraction or "uncovering" of defenses. Paying attention to transference early in therapy and seeing the potential for interpretation derive from Klein's (1932) writings. The approach discussed in this book, however, differs from Klein's: it does not rely on an elaborate and oddly abstract but simultaneously concrete notion of drives and the projection of the death instinct. The approach put forth here allows an everyday, here-and-now relationship between therapist and patient. The therapist can comment on, touch on, but not deeply interpret the "negative transference" early in therapy (Freud 1905a). "You even seem a bit concerned I won't take you seriously if you complain. . . ."

Where and when did this negative self-appraisal and expectation of others originate? Did Mrs. I's parents focus excessively on her superficial compliance without validating or empathically recognizing her emotional life, as some self psychologists might assume? Do her current family and friends devalue her roles as wife and mother, despite her protestations to the contrary, as some social psychologists might suggest? Does her oldest daughter's budding adolescence, as she herself approaches menopause, stimulate guilt about envying her daughter or remind her of her own forbidden and guilty wishes when she was her daughter's age? Does anemia or a thyroid disorder directly alter her affects, coloring how she experiences herself and others? None of these questions can be answered at this time.

There was, however, already information about her ego functioning. She could compare and contrast how she felt about and saw herself with how she *thought* she should feel about and see herself. Her awareness that she usually considered herself successful at her chosen role and normally felt proud and happy enough but that she now felt dissatisfied, unhappy, and less valuable required a capacity to hold two emotional opposites in mind at once. This integrative ego function is often associated with people who have whole object relations, not borderline, split object relations. Mrs. I's ability to experience conflict (here referring to contradictory internal relationships) consciously indicates ego maturity. Although her ego capabilities would be more thoroughly delineated in later sessions, her complex integrative ability already manifested itself; this ability contrasts with the reactions of individuals who have congenital or acquired neurophysiological cognitive deficits. Finally, Mrs. I had been spared experiencing such overwhelmingly destructive interactions in early life that she was forced to excessively divide or split her internal world and to lose the ability to hold contradictory emotional experiences in mind at the same time (Gabbard 1994, Hamilton 1988, Kernberg 1975).

Mrs. I's current psychological structure in object relations terms, then, consisted of a devalued self (although more positive images were remembered), shamed, guilty, and dissatisfied affects, devaluing objects (although caring and approving images were remembered), and ego functioning that was able to modulate, balance, integrate, and differentiate, but that currently confirmed her negative self-appraisal.

While some object relations theorists such as Guntrip (1969) believe that a pure psychology is preferable to an integrated biological-psychological model, modern clinicians cannot risk their patient's well-being by ignoring biological factors, both in understanding the patient and in making various treatment recommendations (Hamilton et al. 1994). Adding ego to object relations units provides a framework to evaluate brain and mental capacities as reflected in integrative ego functioning, not only in dynamic therapy sessions, but also as assessed by formal mental status, neurological, and neuropsychological evaluations.

Biology can also directly influence the affects as well as the ego. Questions about anemia or hypothyroidism remained open. Was Mrs. I experiencing premenopausal hormone shifts? Did "endogenous" or "organic" depression alter her self-experience?

> The psychiatrist listened carefully to Mrs. I's description of herself, her life situation, and her attempts to improve her mood. He noticed that when he empathized openly or directly, she seemed uneasy. She appeared more comfortable with matter-of-fact, clinical demeanor.
>
> After agreeing on another session, the psychiatrist told her he needed records from her internist and her gynecologist. She mentioned that they had done studies indicating she did not have anemia. She appreciated his thoroughness and stopped by the laboratory for thyroid studies to supplement her previously undergone complete blood count and chemistry screen.

In addition to ordering tests to assess possible biological influences on her affects and object relations, the psychiatrist noted that she could accept clinical concern and thoroughness as thoughtful caretaking more easily than she could tolerate emotional attunement. What had led to this characteristic? Did she react like this only during an episode of depression?

During the next several sessions, Mrs. I seemed to enjoy talking and grew less critical of herself for being depressed. Still, she suffered, could not sleep well at night, and wept spontaneously about things she would not usually consider very sad or frustrating. She reported no interest in sex or much of anything else.

The psychiatrist said, "I really think we should see if an antidepressant might help your mood. We can still explore what psychological factors may have led to your depression, but you may get over it faster with a little medicine."

Patient: I suppose you're right. I can't believe this is happening to me. I've never believed in taking pills. I don't even take cold remedies.

Therapist: Needing help is difficult for you, isn't it? It hurts your pride.

Patient: It's not my pride so much. I feel like I shouldn't need help, like it's morally wrong, weak.

The psychiatrist had made an empathic error when he suggested that needing help hurt her "pride." The issue was a moral one for her, not a matter of appearances and vanity. Fortunately she could correct him yet still accept what was correct in his understanding of her: that she had difficulty accepting help. In this object relations interpretation, moral issues like this one do not derive from the "superego." Morality is seen as a function of the entire object relationship, an expectation held by the self-ego-object about how the self should be and act and feel in relation to the object and to others in general. The therapist could not determine at this point the background of her belief that a good person should not require help.

The therapist then explained the risks of, and benefits and alternatives to, medication. He hoped to neurophysiologically help her affects of sadness and her sensation of fatigue. Perhaps her self–other experience, and her beliefs about how much help people deserved, would shift with her mood.

She responded quickly to an antidepressant—a selective serotonin reuptake inhibitor. Within two weeks she felt almost as energetic as before her depression, slept at night, and felt generally good but harried.

> *Patient:* I don't know how I used to do all this. Dan had an early meeting so he couldn't help get the kids off to school. Jenny is such a stall-baby. She wouldn't get ready till the last moment. Then she couldn't find her coat. You know how it is. I was trying to help Billy get his papier-mâché South America in a box so he could take it to school. I had to remind the kids over and over to put their breakfast dishes in the dishwasher. Finally I did it myself, because it's faster. I shouldn't do that. They'll never learn to take care of themselves that way. But I was hurrying so I could get my walk in before the art museum meeting. I had just got my walking clothes on when I realized Jenny had forgotten her lunch, so I had to take it over to the school. There went my walk! It's that way all day long. Last night I had to visit Grandma. Then Mom called to ask me to organize a party for the whole family. I need some stress management skills. I need to start exercising again. Maybe you could teach me how to meditate.
>
> *Therapist:* Perhaps you are hoping that if you take a class or meditate, you can do all this easily without complaining.

Patient: I guess it's ridiculous. If I meditated, I'd have to get up at 4:30 to fit it in. *(Laughing)* Why can't I say "No" to some of these things?

Therapist: That's a good question.

From an ego psychological view, Mrs. I drives herself mercilessly, perhaps to placate her demanding superego and to ward off infantile wishes arising from the id. From a drive theory viewpoint, Mrs. I triumphed over her mother by being a better mother and wife and simultaneously punished her unconscious oedipal striving by relentlessly demanding perfection.

From an object relations perspective, the explanation lies not in the drives, but in the history of her relationships and in the current transference and countertransference. In the transference-countertransference described above, the patient seemed to see herself as ridiculous in the therapist's eyes when he merely intended to mention her perfectionistic demands on herself. He did not comment on the transference at this time, however, but inquired about previous relationships.

Therapist: What did people expect from you as a child?

Patient: I wasn't abused or anything. I had friends and time to play. We had family outings. But my parents were pretty strict, too. "No" was not an option for us kids. I had to clean house and pick my things up. Complaining or whining was out of the question. If we whined, we were sent to our rooms pronto. Mom was big on neatness. Still is. That's why she wants family parties at my place. She doesn't like to mess hers up. She's that way, kinda selfish. I grew up in a house where you took your shoes off at the door and the first Saturday of every month we washed all the windows whether they needed it or not. I always felt like such a loser.

Therapist: Why?

Patient: Because I never felt I could do enough.

Therapist: And you feel that way again, now? Even in the therapy, you feel you should do more, not just take the medicine and talk, but that you should exercise, meditate, take stress reduction classes.

She relaxed for a moment.

Here again the therapist delineated not ego defenses but the here-and-now transference relationship. He commented on characteristic ways the patient felt about herself in relation to others and the rather subtle transference manifestations of being with others. She seemed to see herself as an overwhelmed child placating an excessively demanding and unempathic parent. The only way she earned closeness, approval, and esteem was by accomplishing her tasks without complaint. Paradoxically, her very human needs for emotional understanding and confirmation could be met only if she denied those needs. Since she could find no solution to this dilemma, she could meet her dependency needs only vicariously, by taking care of others without complaint.

As she quickly pointed out, this was not her entire experience growing up. Her mother, father, siblings, teachers, and friends did provide emotional sustenance, but in her memory, in her subjective experience, it was hard earned and rare. As she and the therapist explored her memories and feelings, she began to realize that her excessive compliance might have been the most adaptive solution possible in childhood, but it was no longer necessary.

Patient: Not only do you listen to me complain and not mind, Dan does too. He complains about his work, but he has a good job and isn't going to quit. I don't mind listening to him. I don't know why all these years I thought he wouldn't want to listen to me. Just 'cause I complain a bit doesn't mean I'm going to quit taking care of him and the kids. If I complain to Mom, now, that's another story. I just have to tell her "No."

Therapist: That's still hard for you, isn't it?

By recognizing how hard something new was for her and yet not encouraging her to be able to do it, the therapist provided a new self-other experience for her, an experience of herself as understood and valued, with little attached demand. He implicitly anticipated her accomplishing a developmental task without demanding that she do so.

She had spent several weeks "working at relaxing" and altering her schedule to take her personal needs more seriously. Her predominant view of herself as an inadequate little girl who felt overwhelmed by, and desperate to win approval from, a rejecting and perfectionistic parent altered somewhat. She achieved this change with the help of her considerable ego capacities. Now, as a woman, she needed to take care of her own needs as well as those of others. In therapy she began to see herself as someone who could moderate and balance her own lifestyle.

This change was not fundamental or radical: her primary way of relating remained appeasement of an internalized object by becoming something she was not. She merely added what she considered her therapist's moderate expectations to those she already held. Along with the medication, however, this slight shift helped her mood improve. From the object relations viewpoint, the improvement would not be considered an insubstantial transference cure, but an understandable and important, if slight, internalization of personal experience in the therapy. The fact that she could accept benign interpersonal influence consistent enough with her values indicated flexibility and relative psychological health, not a defensive flight into health.

To this point, therapy dealt primarily with mother–daughter issues. Dyadic concerns about self-esteem in relation to the mother, however, did not remain the sole focus of discussion. Father–daughter and oedipal issues came to the fore.

Oedipal Relationship Patterns in a Woman

Object relations theory does not overlook the importance of erotic and loving longings, competitive striving, and jealousy of and anger toward parents. It describes these issues in relationship terms—self, affect-sensation, object, and ego functioning—rather than in terms of disembodied drives. Every individual can have multiple oedipal relationships. For example, boys as well as girls probably wish for the exclusive attention, including sexual attention, of both the mother and the father, at different times, along with a simultaneous wish to eliminate rivals. All individuals can harbor both heterosexual and homosexual relationship patterns within their internal worlds, although one pattern is usually more predominant. Some patients reveal wishes for the exclusive sexual attention of both parents simultaneously, during ego states when diminished discrimination and increased boundary blurring predominate.

In patients with more differentiated patterns, tripartite relations require the ability to hold two opposites in mind at once. The self may relate in a loving and erotic way to the opposite-sex parent and simultaneously in an aggressive and rejecting way to the same-sex parent. In such a case, ego functioning is highly complex. All people, however, carry within themselves their own nuanced set of oedipal constellations, which can be described individually. Mrs. I's sexual and competitive feelings about her parents were only touched on in her once-a-week therapy over a year.

In the third therapy month, she had begun to feel much less depressed, but nevertheless looked uneasy at the beginning of a session. Her psychiatrist commented, "You seem to have a hard time deciding what you want to begin with this morning."

"I don't know what it is. Things are better. I have time for my walk and even a few minutes to read. I'm sleeping better. I don't know."

"Is there something troubling you right now that you might like to mention?"

Again, when in doubt, this therapist focused on here-and-now emotions in the therapy.

"Therapy seems kind of self-indulgent," she said. "It's like I have this secret place to complain and feel understood. It seems like I shouldn't need it."

The therapist remained silent, wondering what, if anything, to say. What came to his mind was a thought that her mother and father had not been able to provide an empathic self-object function, and so she felt she shouldn't need it. His understanding seemed too abstract, a nonproductive repetition of a previous discussion rather than a useful working through of issues. Why was he so uncertain? Did he have an unconscious countertransference? He didn't know.

"I don't know," she said, musing. "I had a dream last week, but I don't remember it well. Are dreams important?"

"You still wonder whether I'll think what you have to say is important," the psychiatrist commented. He noticed an edge to his voice. Did having to work through her feelings of unimportance annoy him? On the other hand, he mused, perhaps this "secret place" alluded to an unspoken erotic transference and countertransference they both avoided. Perhaps that set him on edge.

"I know you'll think it's important. That's the problem. You might be interested, even if it isn't important. It seems so frivolous. Anyway, I had this dream. I was in a cluttered apartment. It was warm and cozy, but cluttered. It was in a foreign city, perhaps Buenos Aires or some place like that. I was sitting on the bed talking with my old boyfriend during the year I took off from college. That's it. Not much of a dream. It's just that I found myself thinking about him, kind of daydreaming, off and on, all week."

"And this is disturbing?"

"Maybe I want to have an affair. That would be a big problem. Do you think that's what it means?"

He felt slightly anxious, as if her question invited him to confirm or disconfirm, to approve or disapprove.

Understanding people as primarily motivated by their relationships requires therapists to remain aware of their own emotional nuances. A mechanical notion of impersonal drives keeps the subject matter safely and squarely within the patient, especially when the therapist deals with erotic transference and countertransference. A mechanistic theory of internal structural conflict allows the therapist to keep his or her intellectual distance, but a personal relationship theory demands that therapists attend to their own understandable, but sometimes unwelcome, feelings. In treatment, this theory requires differentiation and delineation of the therapeutic relationship that may or may not prove entirely comfortable.

"Perhaps you feel it's not only self-indulgent, but also somehow clandestine and illicit to talk with me about these things."

She became thoughtful and quiet. Then she proceeded carefully and tactfully. "It's not often a woman talks privately, for a long time, with a man near her own age, about her innermost feelings, unless there's romance involved. I've had some fleeting feelings like that about you, but I know you're my doctor. That isn't a problem. Wishing to have an affair with my old boyfriend or someone else and not being able to get it off my mind, now that's a problem."

The therapist considered her statement a sign of a complex integration of her internal and external relationships at the moment. She could allude to transferential and personal romantic, if not erotic, feelings about the therapist and consider them in the context of her relationship with him as a doctor who has a responsibility to help and understand her in a professional capacity. She was becoming more open about her emotional life and her feelings and seemed less compelled to live up to a perfectionistic standard that ignored her emotions and needs. Increased emotional closeness in the therapy, however, suggested the possibility of forbidden erotic and physical closeness, which troubled her.

The alternative approach, interpreting her statement as manifesting the ego defenses of rationalization and displacement to ward off powerful, lustful drives arising from the id and retaliatory punishments from the superego, would have equally explained the material. It would, however, have emphasized impersonal drives, rather than the relationship, as primary. It may have also forced the patient into a theoretical mold that suited the therapist, allowed him distance, and, by ignoring the patient's feelings, thereby recapitulated her early relationships. Very likely the therapist would have subtly conveyed his distant and mechanical understanding to the patient in his demeanor and tone of voice.

"Since that dream, I can't get my old boyfriend off my mind. It's disturbing."

"Tell me about him," the therapist said.

Having touched on the romantic transference and reminded herself of the therapeutic relationship, she seemed more free to talk, to confide in a way she had seldom done. Her thoughts about the dream and her nostalgic memory and current longings unfolded over several sessions. She described a time in her early adulthood that had felt like a vacation from her inner struggles. Throughout high school and early college, she strove to meet high expectations as she had as a child. Later, after marriage, she developed a plan for her life and lived up to her own high expectations. During the year off from college and before marriage, however, she had felt less pressure to excel, as people feel on holidays. Now, at middle life, the demands seemed overwhelming and she wished to escape.

During her previous escape in her early twenties, the social mores of the time condoned self-exploration and self-indulgence in young adults. Her boyfriend showed interest in and accepted her. They talked with one another for hours and had a gratifying sexual relationship. They traveled together. They cared about one another and felt comfortable together, not in an intensely committed way but merely enjoying one another without planning for a future together. She felt relieved when she thought of her mother, with her demands and prohibitions, at a distance of several thousand miles. For the first time in her life, she allowed her surroundings to become messy and felt a naughty joy in it. She and her boyfriend could travel, eat, sleep, make love, lie in the sun. Whatever career ambitions they had stayed on hold.

She was describing, in the above material, a time when she had had a sexual, pleasurable relationship with a man and had enjoyed breaking her mother's rules, running away with him, living in a messy hotel room. This object relationship was tripartite: it included herself and two objects—mother and man. In Mrs. I's therapy, the relationship was internal, at the moment represented by a dream, a memory, and a transference. In the current internal-external transference relationship, the illicit, secret place symbolized the oedipal situation. Perhaps she could attend to such feelings only when she ran off to a different place. Perhaps she felt safe or like a different person when away from her mother and could project her own internal demands and values onto her image of a distant mother.

> After traveling for several months, she and her boyfriend went their separate ways. She felt they were too incompatible to be married: he wasn't ambitious enough to suit her idea of her future life.
>
> Later, her relationship with her future husband flowered passionately. He drove himself much more than had her former boyfriend, and she liked that. They both worked hard but managed to enjoy a few romantic moments together. They planned their future and strove toward it.

Her present dilemma could be understood in terms of personal loyalties and ways, including sexual ways, of being with others. From this viewpoint, what may have helped most in the therapy was the opportunity to discuss her inner life with another person.

> When she returned to the subject of men in a later session, she described her father as a healthy, vigorous businessman. He was athletic and careful of his appearance. He worked long hours and valued money, success, and personal beauty.

He spent most of his nonworking time socializing with his wife and other couples, playing golf, or swimming.

> *Patient:* He was a great guy. Everybody liked him. I remember how handsome he looked at our pool parties. Maybe I had this thing for him. I don't remember that, of course. He liked me. He thought I was cute and used to call me Twinkles, because I twinkled my eyes at him. I always felt good around him, but he was distant, though not emotionally distant like my mother. I mean he was actually not there or was talking with other people, usually women, across the room. I admired him from afar, and he admired me, but he wasn't home most of the time. He worked a lot.
>
> *Therapist:* So you had this sort of wistful longing for the first man you ever loved, kind of like the nostalgic longing you now have for your old boyfriend.
>
> *Patient:* I come here and you understand me and don't put any demands on me. You're like my old boyfriend. I can't run away to Argentina, so I run away to therapy.
>
> *Therapist:* And here you can sit in a cluttered office you don't have to tidy up.
>
> *Patient:* Like the dream of the cluttered hotel room! (*Laughing*) That's right.

She seemed to admire the therapist's mental facility and to feel admired by him, possibly because he remembered the details of her dream from several sessions before, possibly because of a subtle seductiveness in his intuitive understanding.

Mrs. I seemed to have an idealized and erotic transference to the therapist and to bask in his attentive awareness. Therapist and patient now appeared to enact a dyadic father–daughter relationship, a different pattern from the one she had displayed early in treatment. Now she valued herself, the object admired and enticed her, but remained not quite available; her affect grew glowing but wistful, and her ego functions engaged playfully.

The object relations viewpoint agrees with the self psychology notion that such a therapeutic experience of mutual therapist–patient idealization may sometimes be good for patients. Such a dyadic, sustaining self-object relationship in the therapy is not, however, considered sufficient. Explication of the internal oedipal relationship is also important, as a repeated scenario rather than as a drive derivative.

"I really appreciate your help. . . ." She seemed to hesitate, to have a reservation.

"But? . . ." the therapist said, anticipating her reservation and inviting her to explore the other side of the coin of idealization.

> *Patient:* But it doesn't seem very healthy.
> *Therapist:* What doesn't seem healthy?
> *Patient:* It just seems like it would be healthier to be intimate with my husband instead of with a professional.
> *Therapist:* Go on.

The therapist neither abandoned nor rescued her. He did not protect his idealized self-image or become self-effacing. He encouraged Mrs. I to work on her problem with her good ego functioning. In their relationship, his confidence that she could do so and his acceptance of her very human dilemma provided a new experience of self and others, but the relationship itself was not enough. She had to work on the problem.

> *Patient:* It's kind of bizarre. I came in here a few months ago depressed and not interested in anything. Now, I feel better. I can even enjoy sex with my husband, but I don't feel very close to him. I'm thinking about my old boyfriend. And I'm talking with my therapist. It's all divided up. I admire my husband a great deal. He's a great father and good provider—he's regional vice president now.

He's understood my depression and is glad to have me back to my old self. But I don't feel close to him. I can't figure it out.

Therapist: It almost seems as if you have a conviction that if you really love someone, you can't have him. You felt that way with your father, with your old boyfriend, and now you feel that way with your husband.

Patient: (Pondering) I guess I do see it that way.

In this schema an old, internal romantic relationship was transferred onto the current therapy. The therapist did not know whether the glowing report of her husband was an extreme idealization: she tended to idealize others and devalue herself even in treatment. Perhaps her husband was less flexible and emotionally available than she depicted him. If he were as available as she said, why would she act as if he were not? Why didn't she feel close to him?

While the patient worked on the issue herself, the therapist speculated that if her husband *did* respond emotionally, she was unable to take advantage: in her internal world she saw all relationships, including those with both her mother and her father, as emotionally unattainable, and she could not imagine the possibility of a passionately desired and also currently attainable physical and emotional closeness.

Patient: I think he really is interested. But the kids take up all our time. And his new position requires him to travel. We're close, but all we talk about is how tired we are of being busy and away from each other. You know what I really want? I want to travel with my husband. His new position takes him away so much. I'm lonely. I just want to spend some time with him alone. We could leave the kids with our friends. They dump theirs on us all the time, but we never do that to them.

This object relations approach revealed that the primary lack in Mrs. I's life was closeness with her husband. Her previous dream was seen as arising not from an impersonal sex drive, but from a longing for closeness, relatedness, and erotic oneness she felt she could never have. Her sexual wishes and needs were part of her wish for relatedness.

Perhaps she also felt she could not be close because a third party or situation—her mother, other women at parties, her father's job, her children, her husband's job, her therapist's role—interfered. As she felt more accepted in therapy and accepted herself more, however, she began to think about having a fulfilling and attainable relationship.

She used her ego functioning to find ways to make what she wanted happen. She seemed to be doing this first by using her good cognitive skills to actively differentiate her old internalized objects, particularly her father, from her current possibilities. That is, she could see that her husband was available to her, although she had not been seeing him that way. "I want to travel with him," she said.

Relationship with the Oedipal Mother

She began spending more time doing what she found fulfilling, including traveling with her husband. Her sex life improved dramatically. She also pursued her own interests and, although she continued some activities, increasingly turned down requests for volunteer participation at the art museum. She still found it almost impossible to refuse her mother's requests, but slowly began to think that as her mother's demands for cleanliness and obedience had interfered with her attaining a loving, pleasurable relationship in early life, those demands still might interfere with her having time to be intimate with her husband.

Patient: It's hard. If I say "No," she is never going to understand. But if I don't say "No," I have no time to relax or be with Dan or travel or anything. If I don't have the family gatherings, no one will. When my kids were babies, she liked them and would hold them. But once they could walk and mess things up, she didn't want them at her place. It's ridiculous. The woman has a maid! But the fact is, if I don't have her over when she decides, the kids'll never see their grandma.

Therapist: Do you think she was that rejecting with you as a child?

Patient: Probably, when I was a toddler. Who knows? I can't remember that far back. Once I was in school, she took me to piano practice and went to recitals and was proud of me. I liked that. But now, if I don't toe the line, my kids get rejected.

Therapist: I wonder if you can think only of what your children are not getting from your mother and not what you're missing.

Patient: (*Weeping*) She's never going to accept me, is she? (*More tears*) It's funny. I almost feel like someone died. I've been holding onto this idea of what my mother could be like for me if I could only be perfect enough, and now I realize it's never going to happen. It's so childish. I should've got over it years ago. If I want to have my own house, time for myself, raise my kids the way I want, spend time with my own husband, I've got to forget trying to please her.

Perhaps it was no coincidence that she experienced her mother as dying after she began to accept her own sexual feelings and longings to be with an available man. She felt that her mother had not only demanded obedience and been rejecting, but had also interfered with her relationship with her father by commanding his attention and by keeping her busy as a little girl. Perhaps the patient had inhibited her wishes for a man in hope of eventually winning her mother's love. Perhaps she had also wished that her mother would die so she could have her father's admiration, which seemed more attainable than her mother's. When she gave up hoping to please her mother, she seemed to have allowed an old internal image, perhaps of her preoedipal, symbiotic mother, to die or had actively, psychologically killed her. She grieved over this death (Klein and Riviere 1964, Ogden 1986).

The oedipal relationship remains vital in the object relations approach. The Oedipus story becomes another pattern that is internalized and can be repeated. In Mrs. I's version of the many myths about family patterns, the relationship with the perfectionistic mother interfered with closeness to an idealized father.

> *Therapist:* It sounds like you've been keeping your perfect mother alive inside you, in your mind, as something to hope for in the future, when you became perfect enough yourself.
>
> *Patient:* But I don't really need it anymore. (*Quieting down, then with characteristic perkiness*) Well, if I'm not going to get her acceptance and approval anyway, I guess I can do what I want. I can schedule one or two family parties a year, when it's convenient for me, not every time she calls and says she needs one.
>
> *Therapist:* Why would you do that? I'm not questioning your decision. I just wonder what went into it.
>
> *Patient:* I want my children to know their extended family, and I want to keep contact with my family, my original family, I mean, because that's the way I want things to be, for me and my family now, I mean my kids, and husband, and me. I'm not going to get her approval for it. So, if I'm doing it for me, I should do it when it's convenient. Of course, if I tell her "No," she may get spiteful and refuse to come to the next get-together.
>
> *Therapist:* That's the way you felt as a child, that if you crossed your mother, you'd be sent to your room, out of the family.
>
> *Patient:* That wasn't the half of it. She wouldn't speak to me for days. She did the same thing with Dad if he crossed her. But really, she's an old lady. And she's proud of her children and grandchildren. She'll come around. She might miss one party, but not two.

In Fairbairn's terms (1954, Grotstein and Rinsley 1994), Mrs. I's primary mother–child object relations can be described as rejecting and exciting patterns. She experienced herself as an inadequate little girl who strove to appease and gain the approval of a rejecting object by driving herself mercilessly. After adding the ideas of affects and ego functioning used in the model presented here to Fairbairn's, her affects are seen as primarily anxious expectations, and her potentially competent ego function was entirely directed toward accomplishing an endless series of tasks set by the rejecting object. She had little freedom to use her creative thinking to question her own assumptions about how to live a fulfilling life, but remained in bondage to her rejecting internal object.

In secret, however, she maintained a largely unconscious alternative of a mother who approved of her and cared about her. Here she became the adored and appreciated daughter she wished to be. She protected this idealized image of herself and her mother by keeping it secret and separate, split off and relegated to some future time when all her tasks would be perfectly completed. Affects were primarily those of mutual adoration. Her ego functioning was suspended or unnecessary during these fantasy moments of an idealized relationship. Later, when she explored these issues further, she realized she enacted this internal constellation at times by trying to be a perfectly appreciative and tolerant mother for her own daughter. During such times, her ego functioning was directed toward gratifying her daughter and vicariously enjoying that gratification.

Her longing for a perfect, admiring, and erotic union with her unattainable father or other men had striking parallels with this internal and secret, exciting object relationship with her mother. Her relationships with men often seemed dyadic recapitulations of her wished-for symbiotic, preoedipal relationship with her mother. Before her therapy, her feelings about her husband had been infused with wistful longing for that time when their work would be completed, their children grown, and their household in order, when they could actually be together, like her longing to finish her tasks and be accepted by a fantasized admiring mother. And Mrs. I apparently had a similar dyadic, admiring fantasy relationship with the preoedipal father.

Focusing more on her wish for the admiration of an unavailable man, however, conflicted with her wish for her mother's approval. As her therapy quickly shifted from exploring separate dyadic relationships with her mother and father, the oedipal dynamic became more apparent. She then described a pattern of a sought-for father and an interfering mother. The dyadic relationship seemed less important, and the therapy focused on triadic constellations. She began to grieve over losing the once-important, old, longed-for symbiotic mother and father. She developed more complex internal relations in which at least two objects could be held in mind simultaneously, one gained and one lost. Rather than preoccupying herself with the wished-for, nonconflicted relatedness, she recognized that when she gained something with one person, she lost something with another. Recognizing that she could not be all things to all people, and that she did not have to be such a paragon, was a great relief as well as a loss for her.

Mrs. I had been sufficiently successful in her early relationships, education, and work to develop a capacity for conflict toleration in young adulthood. When she became overwhelmed and depressed in middle life, however, both her dyadic and triadic relations needed to be revisited: all people carry within themselves the entire history of their object relations.

As Mrs. I became more aware of her habitual, internal ways of relating to herself and others and of how these patterns had developed in the past and were maintained presently in her internal life, she also began to develop alternative ways of relating, both in therapy and outside it. In the context of an interested and concerned therapeutic relationship, which recognized her feelings and her subjective self as inherently valuable and also recognized her mature ego functioning and ability to struggle with and master difficulties on her own, she could now distinguish largely unconscious internal object relations from her current external possibilities and her own adult capabilities and prerogatives. She began freeing herself from the past without losing its richness. She developed an increasingly complex and mature self in relation to others, along with more refined and gratifying affects; she allowed herself an increasingly free and full use of her potential ego capacities.

This therapeutic work occurred entirely in terms of delineating personal relationships, without reference to impersonal agencies of the mind such as id, ego, and superego. In this fairly mature woman with neurotic symptoms and character structure, the oedipal relationship unfolded as such, a relationship, not a drive and prohibition dilemma.

PANIC AT SELF AND OBJECT LOSS IN A MATURE INDIVIDUAL

Mrs. I's therapy was long and fairly orderly in its unfolding, but object relations understandings can also apply in crisis situations when sudden shifts in external relationships disrupt a patient's life. Here again, the approach looks at internal relationships in the context of current external relationships.

Mr. J, 37 years old, had founded a small company supplying hardware components to larger computer manufacturers. He had been the business and marketing partner, not the inventor or technician. After a merger, he left the company with considerable profit and spent a year investigating venture capital opportunities.

During this year, he spent time with his 29-year-old wife and their 6-year-old son. He helped with housework, cooking, and child care. He had enjoyed helping his mother as a boy and considered his mother more stable and effective than his father. He hoped to travel with his wife and child, but she said she felt overwhelmed by the stress of child care during the years he had worked so hard outside the home. She wanted to take some long-postponed trips by herself.

By the time the year had passed, he had become his son's primary caretaker. He was perplexed that, far from appreciating his help, his wife increasingly criticized his efforts, his appearance, his personality.

Apparently his internal view of himself as a competent male, a nurturer, and a caretaker were largely integrated. His internal expectation of an appreciative mate, however, proved discordant with the external reality as he saw it.

When he discovered, hidden under the mattress, love letters written to his wife from another man, he was shocked, but felt he should have known about the affair. After he confronted her, she angrily left their home, flew to Seattle to be with her new lover, and declared her intention to divorce Mr. J.

He consulted a lawyer who advised him of his options. While he deliberated and waited, hoping for reconciliation and pleading with his wife to go with him to a marital counselor, she moved in and out of the house several times, always leaving the son with him. After three months, she contacted her own attorney and moved toward divorce, then stopped short of filing a court motion. She indicated a wish to take their son with her to Seattle. When the patient reso-lutely objected, she traveled to Cancun with her lover to think about her next action.

Although firm in business decisions, in his marital relationship Mr. J was passive and indecisive. His lawyer advised Mr. J that allowing his wife to leave the state with their son might make seeing the boy very difficult. He might lose his son as well as his wife. If Mr. J believed himself to be the more stable and involved parent, the most certain protection for his relationship with his child was filing for divorce and for custody himself in the next two days.

The next day, his attorney made an urgent call to a psychiatrist who had never seen Mr. J. "He's so anxious, he can't sit still in my office," the lawyer said. "He can't think. He hasn't slept all night. He has a wide-eyed stare. I don't know whether he's having a panic attack or getting psychotic on me or what. Can you see him at the end of the day? He has to make some important decisions tomorrow morning, and he's in no shape to do it. If you can't help him tonight and you have to put him in the hospital, I'll understand. But I'd appreciate your taking a look at him. I'm really worried about him." The psychiatrist agreed to see the patient.

When Mr. J arrived, his voice trembled, but he spoke coherently. He wore a sport coat and slacks and maintained good eye contact. He had no delusions or hallucinations and succinctly provided the history given above. After several minutes:

Patient: I was doing all right. I knew I had to take my lawyer's advice. I even went to sleep okay, but this nightmare woke me up. I suddenly felt wired. It's like I wasn't myself for a few hours. I'm feeling a bit better now. Knowing I had an appointment here calmed me down. And I had lunch with my brother. He understands the situation. He's supportive of whatever I decide. But this morning I couldn't think, and I'm still not all the way better. I was in shock. It was like I'd been shot or something.

Therapist: What was the nightmare?

Patient: I saw my wife on a strange patio. She was radiantly beautiful. She's a very attractive woman, but this was unreal, otherworldly beauty. Beside her was this man I've never met, but in the dream, I knew it was the guy she's been seeing. She said Hello to me, and I pulled out a gun, thrust it in his face, and shot him. (*Shaking his head*) That's not like me. I don't keep a gun. I refused to go to war. I don't believe in violence of any kind. It's just weird.

In the dream a self-image discordant with his usual view of himself had emerged. This dream apparently disturbed him more than had learning that his wife was having an affair.

> *Therapist:* And you've been anxious and unable to think much of the time since then?
> *Patient:* Like I've been in shock. But it's better now.
> *Therapist:* Has it crossed your mind to actually kill this guy?

The therapist needed to determine whether Mr. J's self-disintegration affected the ego functions of distinguishing internal from external reality, controlling impulses, and modulating affect to the extent that he posed a physical danger to others.

> *Patient:* No. I suppose it would be a common enough thought—to kill your wife's lover—except I've never thought that way.
> *Therapist:* Now that it has crossed your mind, you don't think you'll actually do it?
> *Patient:* Of course not. It's not his fault anyway. She's responsible for her own behavior. She volunteered. I hate his guts, anyway, whoever he is. But I wouldn't shoot him. Do you think that's what I'm afraid of?

This patient could be conceptualized as suffering such a severe loss that his self and other, internal and external boundaries, had collapsed into themselves, his ego functioning had been overwhelmed, and his major affect had been panic accompanied by feelings of unreality. The psychiatrist's first step was to perform an external ego function for the patient by clarifying internal and external boundaries, dream and reality, and by inviting his patient to use his own good ego to sort these out. He did this merely by asking questions.

> *Therapist:* Do I think you're afraid of what?
> *Patient:* Of shooting him?
> *Therapist:* I guess that's what I'm asking you.

The psychiatrist had already concluded that Mr. J's conflict was primarily internal and that actual murder was highly unlikely. Nevertheless, he wanted to encourage the patient to assess the situation himself and also to clarify self–other boundaries.

"Even the thought of it is repugnant to me. I couldn't live with myself if I did a thing like that."

The therapist thought for a moment. He didn't like interpreting dreams outright, a technique that often endorses the therapist's ideas over those of the patient and sometimes reveals more about the therapist than the patient. He and Mr. J seemed in a good dialogue, however, perhaps fostered by the urgent situation and raw emotions. He decided to proceed as quickly as this apparently intelligent man could, as long as Mr. J responded with clearer thoughts and decreased anxiety.

> *Therapist:* This is kind of an odd idea, but if you shot him and couldn't live with yourself, it might cross your mind to shoot yourself. In the dream, I mean.
> *Patient:* That's why I felt shot when I shot him? That guy represented him and me? Is that what you're saying? Is that what happens with those people you read about in the newspapers who go off the deep end?
> *Therapist:* It's a possibility. We don't need to come to a conclusion about the dream. I'm just wondering about it.
> *Patient:* Dreams are strange. It makes a kind of sense, though. Just thinking about it makes me feel guilty. It's so uncharacteristic

of me to even think things like that. I can be competitive at business, but. . . .

Therapist: To think violent thoughts, even in a dream, may be like a loss of innocence for you. Perhaps you feel like your view of yourself as a peaceable family man has been shot. It's painful enough to know you've been shot down, so to speak, without dreaming about revenge.

Patient: I have a hard enough time accepting that I won't be a family man. I was going to be financially supportive, help out with the kids, and spend time with my wife. That was how I saw it ever since I was a little kid. Now I'm the housekeeper and taking care of the kid, and she's out running around with other men. Then she threatens to take my boy away. She's forced me into a corner where I have to retaliate. I just wasn't brought up that way. I grew up watching movies of guys rescuing fair maidens. We're supposed to protect women. No matter what. I would've done anything for them. It's really sad.

Therapist: What's sad?

Patient: It's sad for me, because I'm going to lose my wife and my family the way it was. It's sad for her, because she is probably going to lose her kid, unless she can agree to some kind of joint custody and stay in town. And it's sad for Billy, because he's going to lose his intact family.

Therapist: Have you really made up your mind about that?

Patient: I'm afraid so. I decided yesterday. But I think you're right, Doctor, except I think I was really dreaming about shooting my wife. That's a terrible thought!

Therapist: Whoever you're angry at, maybe even if it is at everyone involved, including yourself, this degree of destructive feeling is not something you want to be a part of yourself. It seems to have led you to feel unreal. But you seem to be coming to terms with it.

Unlike Mr. C and Mr. D, who were discussed in Chapter 2, the patient displayed resilience and creativity. Just talking with an understanding person about his innermost feelings allowed him to reintegrate.

> *Patient:* I married someone young and spoiled, then I ne-
> glected her for several years out of my own selfish ambition. I
> suppose I'm responsible for that. But if she's going to run off, I have
> to take care of myself and my son.
> *Therapist:* Have you given some careful thought to what that
> entails and whether you really want to do that?
> *Patient:* Yes, I have.

This therapeutic session was unusual. The speed with which
difficult material came up and was dealt with would not have been
as appropriate to analysis as it was to analytically informed crisis
intervention. Had the therapist given the patient advice or had he
not been so scrupulous about monitoring how quickly the patient
could proceed, the session might not have succeeded. The session
was also unusual in that the patient seemed so shocked by his
previously unconscious murderous self–other experience that his
resulting panic attack overwhelmed his ego functioning, yet he was
not so shocked that he was unable to deal with the issues in a rather
matter-of-fact way the very same day. Mr. J's example illustrates
that, in extreme circumstances, high functioning, well-integrated
individuals can fluctuate in self–other experience, emotions, and
ego functioning in an extreme fashion.

> *Patient:* I don't know why I married someone like that. I may
> be a good businessman, but I haven't made good decisions in my
> personal life. I suppose I've seen women as idealized ornaments, as
> the magazine articles say some men do. It's kind of a put-down,
> seeing women as so wonderful, protected, and incompetent. But
> there's not much I can do about that now.

Mr. J's object relations can be described as shifting from more
to less well integrated, but his usual ability to see himself and
others in a highly complex and mixed way predominated by the
end of the session. His affects were complex. He seemed to feel a

mixture of sadness, guilt, confident determination, love for his son, and regret. His ego functioning displayed a good capacity to work through complex emotional, interpersonal issues. These qualities had probably also helped him in marketing and other business endeavors.

In contrast he also harbored, very likely from childhood, an immature view of himself as a man protecting, helping, and enjoying the favors of an idealized image of feminine beauty and passivity while secretly and largely unconsciously devaluing women as weak and ineffective. His associated feeling in such a relationship was romanticized love, indicated by the dream image of his wife and memories of movies. He himself suggested he also harbored a smug superiority. His ego functions were directed largely toward protecting, pleasing, and politely dominating his "lady" when this aspect of his personality was predominant. As he said in his one session, this relationship must have prevailed when he chose his wife as a partner without taking into account the problems of actual adult life.

From this viewpoint, when his circumstances became so painfully clear that his idealization broke down, he could not deal with primitive feelings of betrayal, abandonment, and rage. His intense emotions seemed to overwhelm his ego functions of thinking clearly in an integrated and differentiated fashion, clarifying self–other boundaries, distinguishing internal experience from external events, and modulating extreme emotions; he panicked. In this state he seemed to lose his feeling of connection with internal and external objects, but to feel disintegrated himself, both shot and shocked. Fortunately, when his relationships and his value as a person were affirmed by his brother, and when he received some help from the psychiatrist in sorting through his feelings and experience of himself and others, his predominantly mature and well-integrated object relations, including ego functioning, returned to the fore. Any such return from splitting, fragmentation, or dissolution of the self may typically be accompanied by sadness and guilt combined with a determination to take constructive action (Hamilton 1988, Klein and Riviere 1964, Ogden 1986).

Oedipal Object Relations in a Man

Perhaps it was his sadness and a need to make reparation that led this patient to stay in therapy, although he never had another panic attack. His therapeutic relationship no longer focused on issues of primitive self-object fragmentation versus fusion, but moved toward oedipal concerns.

> Mr. J retained custody of his child. The boy's mother and her new boyfriend moved back to Mr. J's town, and she was granted visitation rights, with which she seemed content. Once his ex-wife seemed more settled, one root of his dilemma became clearer. He began to feel an intense longing on behalf of his son. He remembered the good relationship he had enjoyed with his own mother and felt that his son was missing something wonderful. He considered "sacrificing" himself and relinquishing custody to his ex-wife and felt an intense and irrational longing to act on this wish. "In my mind, I know it wouldn't be a good thing," he said. "But I can't get it out of my mind."
>
> He reviewed with the therapist his father's being away working much of the time and when home, spending weekends in his office. He had seemed withdrawn and ineffective. As a boy, the patient had kept his mother company in the kitchen, talked with her, helped her with the housework, and done all the outside work. Although his father had made a good living and always seemed kind if remote, the patient remembered feeling contemptuous of him.

He wondered whether he was missing his wife and displacing the feeling onto his son. The therapist also invited him to explore whatever ambivalence he may have had about the responsibilities and time pressures of being a custodial parent. Such ambivalence could have contributed to a disguised wish to give the boy up "for his own sake." What was more compelling to the patient, however, was the idea that he identified with his son and felt tempted to repeat an old pattern with him. He wanted his son to enjoy an exclusive companionship with his own mother, possibly to Mr. J's exclusion. Mr. J could thereby have relived, through identification with his son, the partial oedipal victory he had valued so highly as a boy.

When he thought through his own oedipal relationship and associated affects, he could distinguish his situation more clearly from his son's current circumstances. His longing on behalf of his son vanished. He did, however, negotiate expanded visitation for the mother without jeopardizing his own legal rights and parental relationship with the boy.

More primitive sexual and aggressive aspects of the oedipal relationship did not surface in this series of sessions. The therapeutic approach, however, did not exclude such feelings or relegate them to an unimportant position. While the establishment of self-object relationships is considered the primary motivator of human behavior and emotional life, sexual and aggressive affects and sensations remain major, sometimes intense, aspects of such relationships. Here the oedipal relationship, as in the case of Mrs. I, contained paired affects and objects—the self related to the idealized mother with feelings of closeness and to the devalued father with feelings of contempt—a tripartite rather than dyadic relationship.

In subsequent sessions the patient recalled his dream on the night before he had come to therapy. He associated the dream with his feelings about his mother, his father, his ex-wife, and his son. He began to suspect that shooting the other man had also represented shooting his father and assuring himself an exclusive relationship with his mother as well as with his ex-wife. As a boy his condescension toward his father had also been a way of "shooting him down," so to speak. He became anxious about such a notion, however, because he also loved and identified with his father to some extent and felt "shot down" himself.

In once-a-week sessions with mature adults, many clinicians sort out relationship issues without exploring details of specific erotic and aggressive feelings. Such an approach may be sufficient if the therapist does not avoid these issues because of counter-transference needs. The issue is worth delineating in more detail here, however, to show how oedipal- and genital-level emotions and sensations can be discussed in object relations terms.

In one session the patient said, "I can't get that interested in sex right now. Enough time has passed since the divorce, and I've met lots of divorced women. We talk about raising kids mostly, and I enjoy the company. But it's like hanging around with Mom. It's okay but not exciting. At work I meet single women without children. I have plenty of spare time. I've been lucky financially and have people to pretty much run things for me. Billy is with his mom a fair amount on weekends. I could go out. I just don't."

"What was your sex life like before you got married?" the therapist asked. "You've told me some, but let's hear some more."

He reviewed his young adulthood when he would often have rather intense romantic and sexual relationships that ended after a few months as his idealization wore off. Perhaps he feared such relationships now because their disastrous outcome had destroyed his marriage. He associated these romances with the television movies he had watched on lazy summer afternoons when he was a child. He remembered his mother sometimes taking a break from her work and watching a movie with him. He remembered sinking into the worn couch in the family room and even his mother's faint smell on a hot summer day.

> *Patient:* But that was different.
> *Therapist:* The most obvious way it was different was that the movie women weren't real and your mother was.
> *Patient:* Sure, of course.
> *Therapist:* And your youthful romances didn't quite seem real either.
> *Patient:* As a matter of fact, they were kind of make-believe, kind of "let's play love and have sex." I even thought of myself as in the movies at times. I knew I wasn't, of course, and I knew the other people were real. We both enjoyed it. It really was kind of fun. My ex-wife and I had a great relationship that way and fantastic sex.
> *Therapist:* Until it wasn't a game anymore. Then it was a disaster for you both.
> *Patient:* I would have done a lot better marrying someone more like my mother. Wonder why I didn't?

As illustrated again, a drive theory is not necessary for acknowledging infantile and childhood sexuality.

Over several sessions and mixed with other topics, patient and therapist sorted out his feelings of loving his mother and of being loved by her. He did not remember his earliest childhood sexual feelings, but did remember being surprised by his prepubescent and pubescent responses. Shortly after he discovered he could ejaculate, he began to masturbate while looking at pictures of women in underwear advertisements. Helping with the chores one day, he found himself smelling his mother's mixture of perspiration and perfume on her brassiere while he loaded the washer. Amazed, he found himself with an erection and fled the laundry room. He began to avoid his mother for a year or two.

Therapist: And when you got older you only had erotic relationships with girls like those in the movies and the underwear advertisements, ones who weren't quite real.
Patient: Because they weren't quite real? (*Perspiring slightly*) And my mother and my feelings for my mother were too real.
Therapist: Of course you loved your mother. And when your sexual feelings became more obvious to you, you would have them for the women around you, whom you cared about.
Patient: Do you think that's why I couldn't date women who were solid and competent and stable? Or who had a little body odor that wasn't all washed and deodorized away!
Therapist: Could be.
Patient: I think I'll give it a try. (*A bit naughtily, perhaps counterphobic*) Maybe I've been missing out on something.

This discussion helped explain why he had retained his idealized internal relationships with fantasy sex objects, which he had acted out in his external life with willing partners who might have had reciprocal needs. Perhaps he was protecting his boyhood relationship with his mother, and perhaps he also protected his father from the wishes to castrate and depose him, symbolized by shooting the "other man" in the head in his dream. His dream anxiety about being shot might have indicated that he identified with his father, feared retaliation from him, or both.

This object relations approach emphasizes the need to protect and maintain relationships as primary, not as secondary or incidental to hypothetical sexual and erotic drives or defenses against them. In this example, when Mr. J sorted out his internal relationships and realized that he separated them from one another to avoid their incompatible aspects, he became free to have more mature sexual and loving relationships with women who reminded him of his mother's best qualities and no longer felt he was doing damage to his mother or to his father's memory.

Thus the oedipal conflict does not derive from id instincts defended against by the ego, which creates the superego through identification with the father and his values as a substitute for possessing mother. Neither does the patient's anxiety arise from drive and superego condemnation that overwhelms ego functioning: the oedipal dilemma arises from a relationship problem. Mr. J maintained a self-image as loved and loving and object images of his mother as idealized and his father as devalued. His affect was complacent and warm in regard to his mother and superior, triumphant, and guilty in regard to his father. His ego functions were directed primarily toward retaining these relationships as they were. When erotic sensations and affects erupted in early adolescence, they threatened his comfortable closeness with his mother. He seemed to have protected the idealized mother–son relationship and the equilibrium of an oedipal triangle by creating a new object relationship in which he could have erotic feelings. He saw himself as a gallant man like a movie hero. This pattern probably recapitulated an earlier infantile pattern in his internal world.

With his make-believe women, he could have romantic feelings and erotic sensations, and he could use his considerable ego strengths to enact such a scenario with a willing partner as he grew into adulthood. Such an unrealistic relationship acted out in a marriage, at the same time that Mr. and Mrs. J were trying to bring up their son and he was preoccupied with business, must conflict with the complexities of adult life.

The later part of Mr. J's therapy dealt with the idealized internal object relationships and with his seeing them as now unnecessary. He became free to develop new possibilities, to use his integrative ego functions to bring together elements of his relationship with his mother and of his largely fantasied sexual partners. Part of his maturation in the future would entail letting go of and mourning the loss of his previously idealized gallant gentleman-fair maiden scenario. This loss was not too great: elements of his old, less mature notion of relationships remained in his new and more mature experience of himself in relation to women.

CONCLUSION

The examples of Mrs. I and Mr. J demonstrate that therapists can practice psychotherapy with relatively healthy individuals, who have relatively stable life histories, by using object relations as the central structural pattern and not resorting to id, ego, and superego structures and their implied theory of disembodied drives and defenses. The problems and adaptive capacities of these patients can be discussed in terms of self, object, affect-sensation, and ego functioning—constellations together fluctuating and evolving. Even oedipal issues can be treated as relationship patterns associated with certain affects and sensations and with a characteristic ego functioning for each individual. Conflicts can be seen as existing between experienced incompatibilities in various aspects of the self and others, or among self, affect-sensation, and object. Morality is treated not as belonging to a separate agency of the mind, but is considered a product of the entire object relationship, in which the ego-self compares and contrasts current self, object, and affect-sensation constellations with preferred, desired, or optimal self, object, and affect-sensation groupings.

In the approach described here, relationships become mental *structures* with their four elements always associated with one another. It is this relationship—self, affect-sensation, object, ego functioning—that is structural or stable, in the sense of being repetitively present, but not rigidly fixed. The variations and shifts among differing object relations form dynamic patterns used to describe each personality. In the examples discussed above, healthier individuals, like those less healthy, carry within themselves more mature and less mature object relations. When a fairly mature person becomes stuck or trapped in a maladaptive pattern, he or she develops symptoms. Certain powerful and sometimes primitive object relations can be kept unconscious and secret for long periods of time, yet profoundly influence a person's life.

The four-way pattern of object relations set forth here may be stable and universal, yet each individual's object relations patterns are unique and can subtly shift over time. In periods of high interpersonal stress, emotional arousal, or temporarily diminished ego capacity, these shifts can occur as suddenly and dramatically as the shifts in object relations of individuals with more immature personality development (Hamilton 1992b). This viewpoint allows the therapist to describe what she or he sees at the moment in the patient's internal or external relationships without relying exclusively on one theoretical formulation. The approach is similar to Horowitz's (1992) description of ego states in individuals with posttraumatic symptoms. In this book the object relations theory is integrated with British object relations theory, particularly with Fairbairn's approach, and generalized to include more normal functioning.

If healthier as well as more disorganized people can undergo shifts in object relations, what is the difference between maturity and immaturity? Both the cases discussed in this chapter illustrate that healthier individuals have more complex and modulated self-object images and affect-sensations available to them more of the time. More of their ego capacities are more often activated, and thus they recognize their own good and less good qualities simultaneously and accept these contradictory aspects of themselves. They acknowledge the complexity of their internal and external objects and manifest empathy, compassion, and modulated guilt in relation to others. Their affects are not without passion yet are integrated in complex ways suitable to the complexity of the self-object relationship. The ego becomes creative in differentiating, integrating, balancing, and modulating. In particular, the individual can distinguish self from other and internal from external without sacrificing the ability to identify with, empathize with, influence and be influenced by, and relate to others. When more mature individuals' predominant object relations patterns break down, they usually retain an ability to remember their former, more balanced functioning, unlike many borderline individuals who often forget that they have ever felt and acted differently (Ogden 1986).

Healthier object relationships falter when affects overwhelm integrative ego functions, when toxic or structural brain damage impairs ego capacities, when extreme interpersonal events or life tasks do not correspond with already available ways of relating, and when persistent parental failure of containment and empathy in one area of life has left an otherwise healthy individual vulnerable to one of life's many challenges. (For a discussion of such shifts in relation to splitting and projective identification among healthier individuals, see Hamilton 1992b.)

Although the examples of Mrs. I and Mr. J could have been discussed in ego psychological terms, the patients would have been differently understood according to a theory that is more concerned with mental agencies than with relationships. This difference would undoubtedly have been conveyed, however subtly, to the patient (Hamilton 1990). Similarly, self psychology approaches might have given the therapist a useful understanding of the patient that could have been as personally meaningful as the object relations approach, but would have underemphasized the relative autonomy of the ego functioning and neglected the negative transference to the detriment of a fuller acceptance of complexity in relationships. The advantage of the approach presented here is its flexible and personal nature that does not sacrifice an orderly treatment to the idea of impersonal mental agencies.

5

Approaches to Treatment

Freud (1914, Wallerstein 1992) considered the essential elements of psychoanalysis to be transference and resistance. In object relations therapies, transference interpretation remains the cornerstone. This approach considers resistance an inherent reluctance to give up existing internal relationships, regardless of how currently dysfunctional or inappropriate they are. Relationship theories also acknowledge unconscious mental activity and infantile sexuality as important aspects of human life and development. Consequently, object relations psychotherapies remain psychoanalytic in nature.

These concepts were developed in treating borderline, narcissistic, and schizoid individuals, who require more varied interventions than a neutral interpretation of transference and resistance offers. This approach, however, has increasingly influenced various psychoanalytically informed treatments in addition to expressive psychotherapy. By reintroducing ego functioning into object relations, even more approaches to helping people, some of

them originally elaborated by ego psychologists and child development specialists, become available. In this chapter, clinical theory
is adapted to supportive psychotherapy and general psychiatry, not
only to psychoanalysis or intensive dynamic therapy.

FOUR AVENUES FOR THERAPEUTIC EFFECT

Although systemizing treatment may constrain creativity, an orderly look at options that therapists have available is useful. Because all the elements in object relations shift as any one changes,
defining the aspect affected most directly and intentionally affords
a convenient system for categorizing interventions. Clinicians can
consider directly influencing the self, the affects-sensations, the
internal or external objects, or the ego functioning. Any intervention in one area, of course, has implications for other areas,
especially in that these divisions are abstract and not perfectly
discrete.

Affects-Sensations

Affects

When patients feel depressed or anxious, that emotion colors their
experience of themselves and others and influences their ego
functioning. In most psychodynamic therapies, therapists try to
change affects by addressing issues of the self, object, and ego
functioning. Because psychopharmacology has advanced so far and
combined psychotherapy and pharmacotherapy has become so
common (Dewain 1992, Hamilton et al. 1994, Karasu 1992), avenues for chemically influencing the affects can be considered.

Mr. K, a 52-year-old engineer, complained that he was having a midlife crisis and had recently become disenchanted

with his marriage and work. He awoke early each morning, thinking of life's futility. His previous self-concept as successful and as a good father and husband paled beside his current feelings of worthlessness.

"I don't even love my wife anymore. Lucky I don't find anyone else interesting either, or I'd end up losing my marriage like some guys at work. I feel guilty not loving my wife, and I'm sad all the time."

Mr. K's self-experience coincided with his affect. Did his mood affect his relationships, did his relationships affect his mood, or did they work hand in hand indistinguishably?

> *Patient:* I don't like work either. It's a stressful job. The company markets products before we've quite finished developing them. That's pressure. I'm not really stressed right now. I don't care enough to be stressed out. Two months ago I got so uptight my blood pressure hit the ceiling. I had to start taking medicine for it. But now I don't care.
> *Therapist:* What medicine are you taking?
> *Patient:* Propranolol.

The psychiatrist could have explored how the patient felt about needing medicine and what effect his health had on his self-image at midlife. He could have asked about the patient's youthful daydreams of his grown-up life compared to his present vision of himself. He could have empathized with him. He could have focused on his marital relationship, his boss, his children, or his friends. Instead he asked about something that could directly affect Mr. K's mood—medication.

After determining that his mood had changed when Mr. K had begun propranolol, the psychiatrist told the patient he would call his internist and recommend a different antihypertensive. Mr. K's depression resolved entirely after he stopped taking propranolol, sometimes associated with depression.

"It's amazing that a chemical can do that," Mr. K said at follow-up. "It completely changed my outlook. I had turned into a different person. Now I'm back to my old self. My wife even seems happier. We have our difficulties, but they're nothing like what I was thinking."

Examples of medical side effects so purely and thoroughly affecting one's experience of self and others are not common; more often, psychological, social, and biological causes combine simultaneously. In Mr. K's case some problems at home and work troubled him. He could not deal with those common troubles in his accustomed way when propranolol began to affect his mood. He lost interest in himself, his family, and his work. His ego functions of perceiving himself and others accurately, solving intellectual problems, balancing and modulating affects, and modulating his self-expectations deteriorated, not because of any sedative effect of the medicine, but from his mood of discouragement and not caring. The most salient factor in his shift from usually well-integrated object relations to predominantly depressed object relations was the medication. Consequently the psychiatrist directed his therapeutic intervention directly to the affects and discontinued propranolol. What possible psychological factors may have led this particular patient to have this particular experience of depression remains a separate question.

Other physical factors can affect mood directly. For example, Lewy and colleagues (1987) have demonstrated that the absence of sufficient white, bright light during winter months can cause dramatic emotional changes in some individuals. This mood change can interact with other personality factors in complex ways. The following illustration is more typically complex.

Mr. L, 34 years old, had worked hard for several years to overcome timidity and self-doubt. He had grown up in a family of highly successful athletes. His small stature, childhood allergies, and physical domination by male and female older siblings had contributed to his inferiority feelings. His parents' solicitous praise of his achievements "despite his handicaps" only served to make him feel worse about himself.

When, as a young man, he began to live on his own, education, physical exercise, and self-help books enabled him to reach a middle management position in a competitive business. At the beginning of therapy, he complained that he still got so anxious in meetings that he could not think about anything except how ridiculous he looked to others. He became so inhibited he could barely follow the conversation or speak. He felt the same when he interacted casually with peers and so avoided them. Alone in his office, he always thought about what he should have said.

He considered himself inadequate in relation to competent others, who would ridicule him. Shame dominated his affects. His ego functioning displayed perceptions turned inward until he was unable to recognize how people reacted to him; his cognition was immobilized until he was alone; the affect of shame was unmodulated; actions were inhibited to speechlessness; and he modulated self-expectations poorly. Privately, he held a complementary object relations constellation: he had a secret, grandiose fantasy about who he would be and how he would feel when he finished his perpetual self-improvement campaigns.

One approach to Mr. L's problem would be treating anxiety pharmacologically to see whether medication influenced his feelings about himself and others and his thoughts and actions in others' presence. This approach can prove effective in cases of simple phobia, for example, fear of giving speeches. Since the patient's problems were lifelong and affected every psychic area, however, Mr. L wanted to work on them psychologically. Consequently the psychiatrist first chose psychotherapy as the main treatment.

> Over two years, Mr. L came to understand that he had idealized his family members and devalued himself for defensive purposes. He began to think that he perhaps deified his parents and older siblings and assumed all the blame for his relationship problems in order to hope that he could change himself and join his "perfect" family in the future.

Fairbairn (1943) called this attitude the moral defense. He believed small children so compellingly need good objects for security that it is safer for them to think they themselves are bad and their caretakers good. If people are sinners and God is infinitely good, hope for salvation resides in the Lord. If God were infinitely evil and people good, there would be no hope. This concept has been discussed by several authors (Grotstein and Rinsley 1994).

In Mr. L's variation of the moral defense, he believed that he was the family member with problems, but that he could eventually attain near perfection, like his older brothers and sisters, through self-improvement.

> In therapy, he eventually wondered whether his family members had their own weaknesses and shortcomings that they

and he both attributed to him. He might have carried that burden for the family to protect them and his idealized, internal view of them. Alternative formulations also presented themselves. Perhaps he dealt with aggressive feelings of physical and sexual competitiveness by passively submitting from guilt or by triumphing through failure and not living up to the family ideal. Perhaps he identified with parental and sibling criticism and felt in relationship only when being picked on, at least by himself. Perhaps he elicited scapegoating and domination by peers and secretly felt morally superior to them. He explored all these possibilities to some degree over two years.

Talking candidly about himself with a therapist who understood and accepted his struggles led to significant improvement. He sorted out his early relationships from his current interactions. He began to value his family for teaching him the importance of hard work, persistence, and competitiveness, but recognized that they might have overemphasized these values because of their own shortcomings.

At work he eventually realized his peers were actually interested in what he had to say. His supervisor, in fact, valued his ability to hang back from a business controversy or conflict, then speak his mind, without challenge, near the end of a meeting. He considered it diplomatic, quiet strength, not timidity. His boss had no idea Mr. L spent much of each meeting reminding himself that he was no longer a child, the participants were not his parents or siblings, and he could speak up.

Mr. L apparently shifted from feeling locked in a closed system of internal relationships, as Fairbairn postulated (Grotstein 1994, Sutherland 1989), to a more open dialectic between inner

and outer relationships. Such a shift, however, still took a conscious mental effort on his part.

> In the summer and early fall, these improvements resulted in
> progress at work and a vast advance in his social life. In
> August his sense of humor and playful self-assertion delighted
> his friends and colleagues. He even began dating. By Decem-
> ber, however, he lost nearly all the ground he had gained; he
> became convinced he could barely hang onto his job and his
> girlfriend and was holding on only by not letting anyone
> know how badly he felt about himself. As his mood deterio-
> rated, he returned to the formerly predominant self-effacing
> relationship style. Shame pervaded his life, and his ego could
> not shake this frame of mind.
>
> When the psychiatrist reviewed his notes, he discov-
> ered a chronological pattern and prescribed winter light
> therapy for 20 minutes each morning. This approach im-
> proved Mr. L's mood and allowed him to continue psychologi-
> cal growth during the short winter days.

Did the psychiatrist give up and turn to a new medical
explanation that repeated the childhood allergy approach the
patient's mother had taken? The possibility seemed unlikely to
both patient and psychiatrist. Nevertheless, they needed to discuss
possible placebo effects and the magical wish for cure, as well as
various symbolic meanings of winter and memories associated with
winters.

Was the patient's self-esteem problem always related to seaso-
nal affective disorder and not at all to his family's treatment of him?
The perceived family, colored by the child's affects, projections,
identifications, and cognitive distortions and by the patient's adult
experiences and screen memories, is a complex, debatable subject

like any other issue of historical reality. Would the patient have improved with light therapy alone and without psychotherapy? Perhaps moving to New Mexico could have solved his problems, although it seems likely he would have taken his internal world with him whatever the original causes.

The issue of causation is always complex. Neurological theories, like psychological theories, change over time. Mr. L's case history is not intended to prove that the psychiatrist eventually discovered the correct treatment, but that object relations theory adapted to general psychotherapy and psychiatry allows the clinician to conceptualize a physical approach to shifting affects as a way of influencing self in relation to others.

General central nervous system sedatives, such as benzodiazepines, also influence emotions, especially anxiety, and result in a feeling of well-being. Alcohol can do the same, sometimes bestowing a giddy sense of interpersonal closeness inappropriate to actual circumstances. Unfortunately, sedatives not only affect the mood directly, they also affect ego functions. In higher doses, they interfere with perceptions, cognition, affect modulation, impulse control, even motor control. Being addictive, they also cause craving, which results in a highly valued internal object relationship with a substance.

Antidepressants, on the other hand, cause little ego impairment. They were specifically designed to alter mood chemically even when the cause of disturbance is found in relationships.

Mrs. M, a middle-aged woman, said that there had always been conflict in her ten-year marriage. Her husband had left her, and a month later she entered therapy, at first to show her husband she recognized her contribution to the marital problem, in order to convince him to return. Later she stayed for help in coping with her loss.

After several months, grief turned to full-blown depression. She became socially withdrawn, considered life worthless, and ruminated about suicide. Antidepressants helped her mood so that she could resume seeing friends and getting the social support and encouragement she needed while she continued therapy.

A reaction to external relationships may have caused her depression, but a direct treatment of her affect helped her. The case of Mrs. I discussed in Chapter 4 provides another example of using antidepressants to alter mood, influencing how the patient felt about herself and others and how she used her ego functions in therapy and daily life.

Sensations

This book, and psychiatry in general, emphasizes focusing on affects (Robinson 1995) rather than sensations. Feelings about self in relation to others are the very essence of humanity. Nevertheless, sensations sometimes play an overwhelmingly important part in life. Freud (1923) suggested that "The ego is first and foremost a bodily ego" (p. 26). For Freud, ego as he used it in the cited reference undoubtedly meant *self*; the very core of the sense of self arises from the body and its sensations. Object relations theorists have also commented on the importance of sensations in infantile development. Rinsley (1987), for example, discussed how self-object structures can arise from autonomic-visceral percepts. In his discussion of earliest self-experience, Stern (1985) referred to studies of smell and touch in relation to the parents that showed the child's relationship with others. Sensation has clearly been considered important in infant development. In therapy with adults, however, experience of sensation has been largely ignored, except for studying how psychological experiences can be transformed into somatization, an important topic from the beginning of psychoanalysis.

Even in adults, sensations have an important effect on who people are in relation to others.

Mr. N, a 55-year-old plumbing contractor, shivered as he entered his internist's warm office on a snowy day. He looked in good health and was following up on a cholesterol check.

"I almost didn't come today, Doc. I hate snow," he said. This cheerful and cordial man, who knew his doctor well, developed a far-off stare. His eyes went blank; his whole demeanor changed; and his tone of voice turned monotonous.

"You know I was in Korea. Backin' out of the North after China jumped in, now that was cold. I don't s'pose you know what it's like to be out in the cold that long. I worried 'bout getting shot for a while, then all I'd think about was the cold. Pretty soon, I didn't give a hoot if I got shot, long as it killed me outright. I jus' didn't want to get hit and have to lie down on that frozen ground. I only kept moving 'cause I wanted outa that cold. But it got worse. It was like the cold become parta me. Ice in the wind and on the ground. Seemed like it froze me from inside out, like my bones turned ice. Then, it didn't bother me anymore, like I wasn't hardly a man anymore. I didn't feel it anymore, like I was ice itself.

"I'm a changed man, 'cause a that cold," he said. Then, he seemed to snap back to his old self. "Oh well, at least it's warm now. And you're a busy man. Let's see if we can keep this old ticker goin' awhile longer. How's my cholesterol?"

Just as an affective change necessarily shifts other self-aspects, a sensation can have the same result. In Mr. N's example, the patient described how cold eventually led to temporary dissolution of everything else. His self, objects, and affect-sensations collapsed to one boundless entity—cold. "I was ice itself," he said, as if he were not a distinct entity feeling cold, but coldness itself. His motor movement remained intact—otherwise he would not have survived—but his other ego functions seemed largely impaired. This event changed him forever: he carried cold and dreary blankness within him permanently. His apparent general health and strength allowed him to tell another person about it at times, then to shift out of that state of being at will. A vital ingredient in allowing him to snap out of his all-cold object relations state was actual, present warmth.

What about people with ongoing pain? How can they shift from a self-object state of being overwhelmed by or becoming their pain?

Mr. O suffered from prostatic cancer that had metastasized to his hip and spine. This successful shopowner had faced many of life's challenges effectively and with consideration for others as well as for himself. A young intern, who had just rotated onto the service, asked him if he was in pain.

"Terrible pain. The Vicodin dulls it a bit, and I can nap, but it's wearing. I get mean and don't like anyone else or myself much. I can't be around my wife because I'm such a son of a bitch. Just her being near irritates me. So I stay in my room by myself most of the time."

He described his sensations that led to irascible affect and an experience of not liking himself or others. In this circumstance his ego was placed at the service of withdrawal. His was not a deeply unconscious experience of self and others, but it affected his internal relationships in a way that might have derived from unrelieved pain in early childhood. All people may carry within them unconsciously remembered and felt earaches or stomach cramps, which as infants they might have felt were unremitting. In Melanie Klein's (Segal 1964) object relations theory, Mr. O's pain may represent the bad breast internalized and reprojected onto the wife as representative of the good breast. According to Bion's (1962) system, the patient may have been attempting to manage his pain through projective identification with, and then withdrawal from, his wife in an attempt to flee the unwanted self-object projections. Using Fairbairn's (1954) object relations ideas, one can consider Mr. O's withdrawal into his room as a symbolic schizoid attempt to protect his idealized object from his anger at his wife for not being able to make him feel better. If he did not protect her, he might have had the catastrophic experience of destroying his internal image of his wife as a potentially good object, perhaps precipitating a psychological fall into a "black hole" of nothingness, meaninglessness, and chaos (Grotstein 1990). Mr. O's talk with the intern was not a psychotherapy or a psychoanalysis, and theoretical issues were not sorted out. Nevertheless, the patient's most relevant self-experience could be seen during these few comments. The patient's words also held the key to how shifting his self–other experience could be accomplished:

> Mr. O and his wife and doctors accepted that treatment was unlikely to provide a cure, but they continued to hope. They had a healthy appreciation of his life as meaningful and valuable despite pain, loss of functioning, and economic cost, yet they accepted that his disease would most likely run its course and result in death. They made no further attempts at curative chemotherapy. When the pain grew too great, they used radiation and chemotherapy to shrink his spinal tumor.

A few weeks later, after treatment relieved pressure on his nerve roots, the intern found the patient to be a different man. He appeared calm and relaxed and displayed a gentle concern for others. "It must be hard for a young, active man like you to work with so many patients so ill. You don't need to worry," he said. "It's really not so bad for people like me when the pain isn't bad. I've raised my kids. They're okay. My wife is provided for. We've had a pretty good life. I just feel lucky to have these few months to make my peace with God and myself and to be taken care of by fine young people like yourself."

In the absence of pain, Mr. O returned to whole object relatedness although he continued to be a caretaker. He described himself as able to face difficulty. He could find meaning in life and in his family and friends—his wife, his children, his doctors. His affect seemed one of peacefulness and gratitude.

Unfortunately we sometimes cannot find a medical or surgical solution to chronic pain, particularly in young, otherwise healthy individuals for whom addiction could become a problem. Such was the case with Mrs. P.

Most nights for ten years, this 42-year-old woman dreamed of strange tormentors pursuing her through labyrinthine halls, poking her, pinching her, sticking burning objects into her body. Early in therapy, she drew a picture of herself with spears of pain zeroing inward to the core of her being and radiating outward in bright halos. Glowing pain enveloped her entire existence.

Twice-weekly exploratory therapy soon revealed that the pain reminded her of an aggressive rape she had suffered as an early adolescent. The circumstances of a spinal fracture, which had resulted from a crushing mechanical injury in an industrial accident during young adulthood, reminded her of the rape. Surgeries, braces, and eventual physical therapy seemed like further intrusions. Psychotherapy, in the transference, felt similarly traumatic. When medical doctors and physical therapists became frustrated and ignored her complaints because they could do little about them, she felt neglected by them as she had felt abandoned and neglected by both her parents in different ways.

Dealing directly with the relationship aspects of her difficulties made little headway until the therapist, eventually, seriously considered the possibility that this woman could not improve or significantly change as long as her physical pain dominated her life.

Mrs. P, unlike Mr. O, the cancer patient, had not had a happy early life. She had done fairly well with what good she could derive from her parents until the time of the industrial accident that had fractured her lower spine. Thereafter, pain permeated her self-experience. Insight into how this suffering recapitulated childhood memories of feeling trapped, hurt, and misunderstood did not provide any shift in her helpless and persecuted object relations, her despondent, suffering affect-sensation, and her immobilized ego functions, which centered only on communicating her distress and proving her helplessness.

When the therapist stopped hoping that sorting out intrapsychic and interpersonal meanings of her suffering might alleviate some of it and result in better functioning, the patient did improve a bit. As therapist and patient shifted from intensive to supportive therapy, first weekly, then monthly, she developed a new figure in her nightmares. He rarely appeared at first, but later became a regular feature. He was the benign presence of her therapist, unaffected by her demons, not very helpful, but intermittently present and therefore reassuring. Then she began to expand her social activities and improve her daily functioning a little.

Both patient and therapist considered the treatment a failure in its original goals. She did like to talk to her therapist and felt that complaining helped her bear her discomfort. She continued indefinitely in supportive psychotherapy.

Treatment failures, of course, can be just as instructive as successes. Although it is possible that Mrs. P's early life was so destructive and unmanageable that she would have lived a perpetual nightmare in any case, her ongoing physical pain of traumatic origin very likely contributed to her remaining imprisoned in a destructive self–other experience. If an effective medical or surgical approach to her injury had been found, the therapy may have evolved entirely differently. But all such hopes for cure or for effective pain relief had been exhausted. In such cases, physicians and therapists may be able to do no more than accept that sensations can become so pervasive that doctor and patient may be relatively helpless before them. The doctor can only tolerate helplessness along with the patient.

Ego Functions

An extensive ego psychology, child psychiatry, and child development literature, as well as the entire body of educational research, emphasizes fostering, enhancing, and focusing ego functions. Coaches of young athletes attempt to influence the perceptual, motor, and cognitive functions as well as affect modulation and modulation of self-expectations and expectations of others. Patients not uncommonly refer to their psychotherapists as mentors or coaches.

Even those psychotherapists who practice psychoanalysis as a formal technique directly influence ego functions, although in often unnoticed and undiscussed ways. A simple question following the description of a dream, such as "What comes to mind?" invites the ego function of association. "How did you feel when that happened?" suggests memory of affect, not cognition or perception. The interpretation "When I'm quiet, it seems to remind you of your mother reading when you wanted to play with her" suggests the integrative ego function of comparing and contrasting present experience in the therapy with memory of the past.

This subtle influence on ego functions not only serves as a tool for conducting an analysis, it influences the patient. Unlike psychoanalysis, the attempt to mobilize ego functions is obvious and direct in many psychotherapies.

> Ms. Q, a woman with dissociative disorder, complained to her therapist, "After sessions, I get so upset, I wander around in a daze for hours. I have to take the whole day off and can't go back to work."

Something about the way therapy was being conducted, not just the content of discussions, may have interfered with her thinking. Fortunately her therapist responded to her need.

> "Perhaps when we talk about things that distress you, you need the last few minutes at the end of sessions to compose yourself. Would you like to try that?" the therapist asked.

Composing oneself can be considered the ego function of affect modulation.

Not only did the therapist suggest that the patient engage this ego function, she began to initiate it herself by looking at the clock toward the end of the hour. "Perhaps we should spend a few minutes winding down," she would say. Then they would talk about daily activities and the patient's schedule for the rest of the afternoon. Soon the therapist merely looked at the clock from time to time to pace her own comments. The patient would calm down, compose herself, and begin thinking about her everyday activities.

In ego psychology, the setting aside of disturbing memories, fantasies, or emotions is the defense mechanism of suppression. Unfortunately, defense has come to connote something artificial and superficial, whereas conscious awareness of powerful emotion is often seen as somehow more genuine and true. In the object relations approach presented here, *suppression* means conscious and active setting aside of something disturbing and deciding to attend to something else temporarily. The underlying mechanism is not suppression of a drive or impulse, but a cognitive effort to shift attention. The self-ego purposely shifts object relations state or frame of mind.

Several weeks after her therapist began timing the intensity of sessions, Ms. Q once again found herself discussing a disturbing set of memories and fantasies.

Patient: I feel betrayed by everyone. It just keeps happening over and over. When my teacher seduced me into a lesbian relationship, my mother knew I was spending too much time with her. Didn't she wonder why?

Therapist: So you felt betrayed by both of them.

Patient: Yes I did. And then I got involved with that hypnotist. I don't know whether he made up that stuff, psychologically screwed me with his own sexual fantasies that I thought were my memories, or whether he was right about those fantasies actually being memories of abuse. Anyway, he couldn't help me.

Therapist: Like your mother couldn't help you and you're afraid I can't help you.

Patient: Yes, but we only have a few more minutes, and I know you can't help me all at once. In the meantime, I have to make a living. We can talk about this some more next time. Right?

Therapist: Right. What do you have going this afternoon?

The patient, in a somewhat confusing way, described herself as feeling helpless and betrayed by people who either exploited or neglected her. The therapist commented on part of the transference expectation by saying that the patient felt that she, too, could not help her. One can call this the betrayed object relationship, which seemed to dominate Ms. Q's life. The therapist postponed the other part of the transference, Ms. Q's expectation of being sexually exploited, either physically or mentally, by the therapist.

The patient may have been reassured by the partial transference interpretation. It alone may have shown her the distinction between remembered relationships and her current life, thereby helping her calm herself. Since the therapist had spent several weeks stopping sessions and encouraging the patient to think about her benign daily activities until the next session, however, the patient very likely was beginning to identify with her psychologist's structuring. As she engaged her ego, she shifted from a helpless, betrayed object relationship to an image of herself as an effective person who could focus competently on her activities in safe work relationships.

Describing ego functions and the self separately, as if they are different, may be misleading. Perhaps it is better to describe the patient's effort at the end of her session as a volitional activity of the self. Nevertheless, it is important to have some terminology that helps therapists step out of the emotional position in which they find themselves vis-à-vis the patient and consider the patient's autonomous and constructive activities in relation to tasks, not necessarily highly emotionally charged objects. When the therapist values the patient's ability to temporarily let go of preoccupation with destructive internal-external relationships and accomplish useful tasks, that therapeutic attitude can be confirming and useful to the patient. The therapist can convey a valuing of their activities merely by asking about them rather than relentlessly focusing on the emotions.

Having a separate word for traditional ego functions provides a framework for carefully discriminating among the particular mental activities. This therapeutic intervention becomes vitally important in dealing with issues of remembering, as in a further example from the case of Ms. Q.

> *Patient:* I get so confused about my previous therapy. I don't know what happened. I know what happened with the teacher. But then, after hypnosis, I began having all these eerie feelings. I saw this image of someone hovering over me. I felt a piercing pain in my bottom, like my rectum being torn.
>
> *Therapist:* Since the memory of your teacher seems ordinary, what makes it seem that way and not a fantasy?
>
> *Patient:* I was an adolescent. I remember all the events around it. I had a friendship with her. I remember her in class and where she lived and everything that led up to it. I also remember having this memory off and on throughout adolescence and adulthood.
>
> *Therapist:* What makes that different from what happened in hypnotherapy?
>
> *Patient:* It was weird. I just had this image and this feeling out of nowhere. It wasn't connected to anything at all.
>
> *Therapist:* So it was a fantasy?
>
> *Patient:* Yes, but I'm not sure if it's connected with an unconscious memory or not.

At this moment in treatment, the patient did not so much remember or fantasize as think about her remembering. She seemed to have an actual memory of a relationship with her teacher. The memory had clarity, context, and continuity. She also remembered her hypnotherapy and the associated fantasies and feelings. This experience seemed more an internal perception, an immediate vision and sensation, than a clear memory. There was no context in terms of time, surroundings, other events, or any other external referent. This lack of contextual continuity charac-terizes fantasies and dreams, that is, internal perceptions. The distinction between the ego functions of internal perception and memory may not always be clear, of course. Sometimes memories arise vividly. Some people can visualize paintings, faces, even numbers on a page. Others can hear songs and tones of voice when they recall them. Although internal perception and memory may overlap, it remains important for therapists to have concepts for these distinctions in order to understand their patients and try to make sense of their experiences. Ms. Q continued.

> *Patient:* Maybe I'll never be able to know. I don't think you psychologists have even figured out how to tell when memories are true.
> *Therapist:* It's a complicated topic, but for you it isn't just an academic interest. Living with this uncertainty makes it hard for you to feel safe with other people.

The therapist shifted from focusing on cognition and the ability to tolerate uncertainty to the patient's relationships, "feel-ing safe with other people." At this point, the patient seemed reassured that psychologists, including her therapist, had to toler-ate uncertainty, too. Once the patient felt safe and not cognitively confused, the therapist shifted back to the relationship aspects of dysphoria, which uncertainty elicited in her.

Unlike dynamic therapies, behavioral, cognitive, and psychoeducational treatments almost exclusively address ego functions and pay less attention to emotions and internal relationships. The psychiatrist at the Menninger Clinic, described in Chapter 2, did this when he encouraged his depressed patients to keep a regular schedule of work and exercise. Nurses who orient a demented or delirious patient assist their ego functions. Occupational therapists, who help schizophrenic patients take cooking classes, provide the same service. Just as helping professionals must attend to the relationship implications of their interventions intended to aid or encourage ego functions, dynamic therapists must recognize the importance of autonomy, of volitional aspects of the self, of the self's ego functions, while they attend to internal relationships and feelings.

Pharmacologically, the ego function of regulating cognitive and perceptual attention can be affected by methylphenidate and other stimulants. These directly influence the affects as well. Neuroleptic medications have complex effects on the ego functions, enhancing some and interfering with others. Central nervous system sedatives, in sufficiently high doses, interfere with most ego functions. The details of pharmacological influence on ego functions, however, are beyond the scope of this book, although it is important to recognize that pharmacology has an influence.

Objects

Individual psychotherapists do not deal with a patient's external objects; such intervention belongs to family or group therapy, social work, family education, and so on. Patients bring to individual treatment their internal worlds, described and played out in the context of talking with the therapist. For this reason, object relations psychoanalysts, such as Kernberg (1992), emphasize the here-and-now transference. The moment-to-moment transference relationship comes alive in therapy and provides an avenue for helping patients change their feelings about themselves in relation to others. In addition to the transference relationship, however, therapists and patients also find themselves in what Greenson (1971) calls the real relationship and Adler (1985) calls the personal relationship.

In the object relations approach, two primary ways of influencing disturbed and disturbing internal objects present themselves. Therapists can interpret transference, and they can serve a containing function in the personal relationship. An attempt to cognitively manipulate various internal objects without attending to the transference seems futile at best and dangerous or destructive at worst.

In drive theory, transference is considered the transfer of drive energy from the original object to the analyst. In object relations theory, it is the transfer of an internal set of relationship expectations and feelings onto a present, external relationship. Interpretation distinguishes internal or past relationships from external or present relationships.

Mr. L, the 34-year-old patient described earlier in this chapter, had lifelong inferiority feelings in relation to his athletic brothers and sisters and later to his peers at work. His therapist first attempted to help him by distinguishing his internalized childhood interactions with his siblings, who ridiculed him, from his actual external socialization with co-workers. Mr. L could hypothesize, along with his therapist, that perhaps his colleagues did not look down on him in disdain, but this intervention had no emotional power for him.

The therapist's approach did deal with transference in the sense of the patient's transferring emotions relevant to his siblings onto his peers. Since it was not group therapy or workplace systems intervention, the peers were absent, at the moment, in the therapy. Only the patient's report of his internal world was present. Consequently, the therapist might have been encouraging the ego function of cognitively differentiating Mr. L's past with his siblings from his current relationships with co-workers. He might also have been trying to manipulate or influence the perception of two internal sets of object relations. Although this approach might have helped in a way, it did not prove powerfully moving to the patient. In retrospect, it might even have subtly reinforced the transference in the room at the moment by implying that the therapist, like the older siblings, felt superior to the patient, in that the therapist thought he knew how the patient should see things. Eventually this transference became more pressing.

> Mr. L again described how humiliated he felt after making a comment in a business meeting. The therapist asked, "Are you sure your colleagues were as scornful as your brothers and sisters were?"
>
> Mr. L replied, "You keep saying that. Maybe you think I should just have confidence and everything will be okay. You get along with your colleagues. You probably play golf on weekends and ski in the winter and have lots of friends. It's easy for you to have confidence, but it's hard for me."

Mr. L may have noted impatience in the therapist's tone in their "real relationship." He did not, however, know very much about the therapist's personal life. Mr. L's description of his therapist was strikingly similar to that of his siblings and was thus colored by transference. Even if the depiction of the therapist somewhat corresponded to the actual person, the patient's reaction seemed driven by an internal relationship. Emotionally charged at the moment, the patient felt weak and devalued in relation to a superior and idealized object, the therapist. The relationship, now active and alive, could be influenced through transference interpretation and containment. Emotional power resided in the moment. It hadn't been there when doctor and patient, at arm's length, discussed problems at work.

> The therapist said, "Perhaps you have the idea I'm a popular athlete, like your siblings, and I'm telling you to 'just do it.' "

By pointing out the transference, the therapist invited the patient to develop insight, to learn that he saw people as internal objects, when they were most likely different. This insight alone could help the patient, but it would not actually change his internal object relations. The value of the transference between therapist and patient derives not only from its palpable immediacy, but from the possibility of actually changing the internal relationship by responding differently than the patient expects. What the patient had once externalized he could now reinternalize in somewhat altered form. The therapist tried to understand the patient emotionally rather than command him to "just have confidence." This therapeutic stance created a new way of being with others for the patient, an experience that is the containing aspect of transference interpretation.

Bion (1962) coined the term *containment* to describe the parental and therapeutic activity of empathizing with and internalizing an emotional experience, psychologically metabolizing it, so to speak, transforming it, giving it meaning, and returning it to the other in the form of a comment or behavior. Although Bion originally described it in terms of projective identification (the externalization of self), it is equally applicable to transference (the externalization of objects). To some extent, transference and projective identification are artificial distinctions, because in object relations, self and object are always paired and sometimes interchangeable.

In Mr. L's example, the therapist performed a containing function by understanding while not conforming to the role expectation of his patient, not accepting the patient's idealization of the therapist as one who knew how to "just have self-confidence." He attempted to understand him emotionally.

> "I guess maybe I don't know for sure," the patient responded, "but you seem pretty self-confident to me. And that's okay. I wouldn't want some loser to try to help me."
>
> The therapist sat back in his chair. He felt perplexed and stymied for a moment. Then he said, "Perhaps you'd actually rather see me as confident and effective, because that way you think I might be able to help you. But if I am that way, you think I look down on you and that I see you as a loser."
>
> "Right, that's what I grew up with," he said. "I was stuck either way." He went on to describe several examples of interactions with siblings. He had never believed that people who felt confident themselves could also be confident in him. The therapist, however, did display confidence that the patient could work through this problem, confidence expressed in his tone of voice and demeanor.

The therapist's confidence in the patient can be considered part of the containing process. In a previous publication, I described it as the analyst's benign projective identification (Hamilton 1990). It can also be considered an aspect of the real or therapeutic relationship (Greenson 1971). The literature on this subject, beginning in the 1950s, has become voluminous. Today most psychoanalysts, whether or not they ally themselves with an object relations school, acknowledge that the therapist affects the patient's internal world to some extent by serving as a new, outside object that is internalized, if only in the form of the analyzing function itself.

Sometimes therapists may attempt to act as a new or alternative external caretaking and valuing object in more direct ways. In supportive treatments, the therapist may encourage, praise, advise, criticize, or help the patient. This practice can be useful at times and at other times can become treacherously complex. The therapist's attempts to directly help a patient can have unintended meanings. A therapist may inadvertently repeat patterns from the patient's past in an unhelpful fashion. For this reason, many clinicians find supportive therapies more complex and challenging than they do expressive ones.

> Mr. R, a businessman, came from a prominent family. His stoic and moralistic parents ignored both affects and physical sensations in themselves and their children. They favored firm if subtle decorum.
>
> In one session, he did not display his accustomed ease in talking. He discussed business interactions and family life with a distracted air and shifted in his seat. His complexion looked pale.
>
> "Are you uncomfortable?" the therapist asked.
>
> "Oh it's nothing. We were on the boat yesterday, and I twisted my back."
>
> "Would you prefer to sit in that chair?" he asked, pointing to a firm desk chair. "The one you're using is awfully soft. It's terrible for people with sore backs."

The therapist acted like someone who cared about attending to the patient's physical comfort, not just understanding his feelings.

His comment was supportive. The patient could have taken the remark as concern, in marked contrast to his parents' style. Nevertheless, in itself it probably did not help him very much. As a successful man, he was used to people treating him considerately, and such treatment had not changed his inner life.

In addition, however, the patient had a transference to the therapist whom he saw as somewhat stoic and moralistic like his parents. Attention to his feelings, both emotional and physical, reminded him that he could be understood and accommodated by someone he deemed parental. This factor gave the therapist's offer some emotional meaning. It could have also seemed an affront to the patient's pride or coddling, an opportunity to evade other painful realities, a compromise in the therapy, or a dominating and patronizing move. It was not clear what this offer meant to the patient.

Mr. R declined to move. "Oh, I'll be all right here," he said.

"You seem uneasy with my noticing your discomfort and offering you a different chair," the therapist said.

They discussed parental reactions to his physical and emotional life. While he felt proud of his ability to ignore pain and appreciated his parents teaching him that, he felt a bit ashamed of his secret wishes for sympathy.

At session's end, the patient said, "Perhaps you could refer me to someone about my back. I wasn't able to sleep last night." This gentleman would not have asked his psychiatrist for muscle relaxants or narcotics. He was much too aware and respectful of roles, but could allow his psychiatrist to provide him a referral. The psychiatrist did so.

Offering to actually help the patient, rather than just notice his discomfort and his hesitance to mention it, changed the therapy in unforeseen and as yet unexplored ways. In this case, it eventually worked out well, but this is not always the case.

In the example of Ms. S, direct help actually stymied the treatment.

> Ms. S repeatedly complained to her therapist, a male psychologist, that her husband dominated and controlled her. She felt humiliated by his tightfisted approach to family finances, although she earned more money than he did. He demanded sex in ways disrespectful of her feelings. She believed he punished the children too severely. She repeatedly threatened divorce when angry, then retracted it. He also threatened divorce at times.
>
> "Since you frequently think about divorce yourself and fear he might leave you, perhaps you should talk with an attorney to find out what it would mean in a practical sense," the therapist said, thinking the patient would feel less frightened and helpless if she knew her actual options.
>
> The patient misinterpreted his advice and concluded the therapist had recommended divorce. She thought he did not understand the value of commitment. Therefore, she said, she could not trust him. She did not return to treatment.

In this instance, Ms. S did not perceive as helpful the advice of the therapist, but saw it as his own lack of commitment. Helping through containment and transference interpretation seems much more predictable than attempting to take on the role of a practical helper, although such assistance is certainly within the role of a supportive therapist.

The Self

Influencing the self separately and directly seems logically impossible at first sight. The therapist is an outside object, as any third-person observer would readily acknowledge. A separate person influences the patient's subjective sense of self through affect-sensations and ego functioning. In all object relations theories, however, self and object can be recognized as interchangeable to some extent. A varied terminology has evolved to describe this blurriness of who is who, even in healthy and fairly well differentiated individuals. Related nuances of this complexity have been called the interpersonal field (Sullivan 1953), selfobject (Kohut 1971), dual unity (Mahler et al. 1975), symbiosis (Mahler et al. 1975), self-object (Hamilton 1988), and intersubjectivity (Stolorow et al. 1992). Projective identification (Klein 1946), containing (Bion 1962), and empathy (Kohut 1971) have been considered the mechanisms of this interpersonal and self-object fluidity.

> In the earlier example of Mr. L, the patient said he wanted the therapist to be confident, like his siblings; otherwise the therapist would be a loser and couldn't help Mr. L. At that moment, the therapist felt perplexed and stymied. To elaborate on that moment, the therapist empathized with what it must have been like for the patient as a boy. He looked within himself and noticed his sense of being perplexed and checkmated. The boy must have wanted to look up to his older siblings, to learn to be like them. But if he did look up to them, he had to agree with their condemnation of him as weak and inferior. The patient himself must have felt confused and cornered.

Empathy has been thoroughly and complexly defined (Lichtenberg et al. 1984). It can serve as a way of putting oneself in the emotional position of another or of introspecting as a way of understanding someone else. Either way, the therapist feels that his or her emotions are the same, or somewhat the same, as the patient's. Unlike fusion, no complete loss of personal boundaries occurs. Empathy is a sense of being separate yet the same.

In the instance of Mr. L, empathy occurred spontaneously. The therapist suddenly felt perplexed and stymied before he had any cognitive grasp of how this feeling had arisen. When he conveyed his empathic insight to the patient, Mr. L felt understood. "Right, that's what I grew up with. I was stuck either way."

In the previous section's discussion of objects, this interaction was considered as transference. In self psychology, because the therapist empathizes with the patient and conveys that empathy, he performs a self-object function. The therapist sustains and values the patient's self for him. Such an intervention can be called a self-object function: while the therapist remains an external object, he performs the self-function of introspecting and recognizing feelings on behalf of the patient. If the patient accepts this empathy by feeling understood, his sense of self and self-esteem can be directly affected by the therapist. Stolorow and colleagues (1992) elaborated the related concept of intersubjectivity, which is based on self psychology and provides a similar theory for understanding how the therapist directly affects the patient as a self-object.

No inherent contradiction exists between considering comments as both transference interpretation and self-object function. They are related aspects of the same intervention. As transference interpretation, the therapist points out that the patient experiences him, an external object, as if he were an internal object representation of his siblings. As self-object, the therapist introspects as a means of understanding how the patient might feel in relation to his internal objects and in relation to the therapist. One can be self and object simultaneously.

While emotionally powerful, a self psychology approach can overemphasize the self–self interaction and blur psychological boundaries in the mind of the therapist, as if mind reading or telecommunication were occurring. An alternative understanding, although more complex, describes self–self interactions in therapy and recognizes interpersonal boundaries more clearly. This formulation relies on the concepts of the projective and introjective identification.

When Mr. L's therapist suddenly felt perplexed and stymied, he could have thought the patient had put him in an insoluble dilemma and been annoyed with him for foiling his attempts to help him in a competent and confident fashion. Instead, the therapist reacted by wondering if his own feeling of being trapped might correspond with the patient's feeling. Using the projective identification concept, the therapist might have speculated that the patient projected an unwanted self-aspect (the perplexed and stymied little boy) onto the therapist and simultaneously behaved in such a way as to elicit those feelings in him (Gabbard 1989, Grotstein 1981, Ogden 1982). According to this formulation, Mr. L caused the therapist's feelings by arousing contradictory expectations, until the therapist felt caught in a confusing dilemma. The therapist internalized the projection and identified with it, came to terms with it, and altered it by returning it as an understanding of a difficulty rather than as proof of inferiority. Bion (1962) called this process of internalizing, metabolizing, and returning a projected affect and self-experience *containment*.

When the patient accepted the therapist's understanding, he in turn reintrojected what he had previously projected, now altered by the therapist's confident expectation that the dilemma could be understood and tolerated. If the patient identified with the therapist's understanding and confidence as he seemed to, his self would be altered, either slightly or significantly, by this circular process of projective identification and introjective identification called containment.

At the time the patient experiences introjective identification, the therapist engages in projective identification (Hamilton 1990). He projects his confidence that the difficulty thrust upon him is understandable and either resolvable or sustainable onto the patient and identifies with that feeling in the patient. When Mr. L engaged in projective identification by projecting an aspect of himself (the stymied little boy) onto the therapist, the therapist engaged in introjective identification.

Using the concepts of projective and introjective identification, therapists can hypothesize a direct effect on the self, at least metaphorically, through the process of exchanging aspects of the self. Therapists may find using the containment concept preferable to relying on the ideas of empathy and self-object function alone. The containment concept provides for conceptual clarity of interpersonal boundaries. Any of these concepts, however, although therapeutically powerful and emotionally compelling, must be applied with some sense of uncertainty. If the therapist becomes too convinced that empathy or introjected feeling belongs to or arises from the patient, enmeshment can result. The therapist may misattribute feelings in a way damaging to the patient's sense of self, with the result of feelings of alienation, confusion, lowered self-esteem, or, more dramatically, worsened dissociative states. As a corrective, therapists must be open to revising their intuitive sense of what is happening with the patient and express a confident expectation that the patient can come to articulate his or her own feelings accurately.

CONCLUSION

In my version of object relations theory, the therapist can focus on various therapeutic avenues for helping patients. While each approach emphasizes different aspects of the person, each intervention affects the whole person. A transference interpretation, for instance, influences not only how patients experience others, but also how they experience themselves, how they feel, think, and act. Transference interpretations remain the central element of this dynamically informed psychotherapy.

At one time, many psychiatrists reserved attempts to treat affects pharmacologically to situations in which psychotherapy alone could not reach a patient whose affects overwhelmed the ego. The effectiveness and public acceptance of antidepressant and antianxiety medications have increased so much that now psychiatrists often feel obliged to offer these treatments early, when first discussing the risks, benefits, and alternatives to treatment. Medications, however, can complicate the relationship and the transference. Does the patient experience an offer of medication as helpful and understanding, as demeaning, or as confirming an inherent flaw? From an object relations perspective, medication issues can become extraordinarily complicated, as my colleagues and I have discussed elsewhere (Hamilton et al. 1994).

Influencing ego functions directly through educative or other techniques runs the danger of ignoring transference and projective identification in important ways. Such attempts may also become controlling, patronizing, or out of tune with the patient's emotional subjectivity. Nevertheless, awareness of the patient's ego state and inherent limitations in cognitive and perceptual-motor capabilities must be taken into account when making therapeutic interventions.

Self–self interactions can blur self–other boundaries, ignore ego function limitations imposed by brain neurophysiology and structure, and overemphasize the subjective at the expense of everyday reality. Yet such interventions may prove intuitively subtle and emotionally powerful. They sometimes provide the only avenue of approach to a patient, and they probably always occur to some extent, whether therapists attend to them or not.

Although this conceptualization of object relations as composed of four elements can promote the misconception that a person is not a unitary entity, it provides a framework for acknowledging various aspects of the person without ignoring one or the other. From a different theoretical perspective, Beahrs (1982) calls this approach "unity and multiplicity."

6

The Theory

The object relations theory I present in this book differs from or adds to previous conceptualizations in four ways. First, the theory reintroduces ego functioning into object relations. Second, instead of searching for basic or primordial object relations, it describes patterns in current, individual experiences and thereby allows for infinite variability while acknowledging certain themes as common. Third, the theory describes shifting of states of mind from moment to moment. Fourth, it recognizes the self in relation to others as an entity that evolves throughout life as well as from moment to moment.

Previous chapters have focused on clinical applications of these elaborations, but this chapter addresses some theoretical issues. Every clinical practice necessarily implies a foundational theory, and examining the history of these underlying assumptions can be very fruitful.

This chapter was adapted and expanded from Hamilton 1995, as printed in the *Bulletin of the Menninger Clinic*.

OBJECT RELATIONS PATTERNS

Freud's genius created a humane, accepting interpretation of who people are, how they think and feel, and what motivates them. His psychoanalytic technique gave patient and therapist alike a new freedom to explore memories, dreams, and feelings about self and others. He provided an understanding of personal interchange between internal fantasy and external relationships via transference, projection, and identification.

Freud's psychological theory, derived from his personal experiences on the path to self-discovery, necessarily relied on the mechanical abstractions prevalent in Western thought during the nineteenth century. For example, he (Freud 1905b) used nineteenth-century biological notions of instincts to describe the aims and objects of drives: drives arise from inside the subject, and the object becomes meaningful only when invested with libido as a result of gratifying the subject's drives (Brenner 1973). Such positivistic and linear causation theories characterized scientific and medical thinking from the nineteenth into the early twentieth century. In Freud's theory, relationships were no more than incidental by-products of drives.

Fairbairn (1954) disagreed with Freud's views and considered the infant inherently related to the object from birth. (Along similar lines, Winnicott [1965] declared, "There is no such thing as an infant" [p. 39n]. He meant that a baby cannot exist in isolation, but only in relation to its parents [Stolorow et al. 1992].) He went on to develop a clear understanding of self related to objects, a theory not entirely reconcilable with drive theory (Greenberg and Mitchell 1983). Discarding the mental structure of id, ego, and superego and replacing them with his own structures, Fairbairn describes a central ego related to a central object, a libidinal ego related to an exciting object, and an antilibidinal ego related to a rejecting object. These relationship elements structure the personality. Energy pertains to the self as libidinal or antilibidinal rather than to a nonpersonal drive repository, the id. Sutherland (1989) recognized that Fairbairn's interpretation of ego corresponds to a large degree with the current United States term *self*, as used in self psychology and elsewhere. Fairbairn did not direct any attention to formal ego functions as described by Anna Freud (1936) and Hartmann (1964).

For years, neither Fairbairn's theory of libidinal and rejecting objects nor Klein's ideas about the good and bad breast had much currency with United States ego psychologists, although the British middle school (King 1983) accepted and debated them. When U.S. interest in borderline disorders emerged, however, the marked changes in self–other experience these patients undergo were shown to be explained by object relations concepts. Kernberg (1975, 1976), Masterson (1976, Masterson and Rinsley 1975), and Rinsley (1978) each described all-good and all-bad split object relations units found among these patients.

These units are not really units, but states of mind associated with self, affect-drive, and object. This spare and excessively discrete description of "units" appealed to U.S. clinicians with their penchant for catchy terminology and readily graspable, prepackaged concepts. They could readily discuss such phrasing and fit it into medical and psychological literature without recourse to the fluid essay style of British, European, and South American thinkers that was replete with complex, ever-changing combinations and permutations of meaning. Nevertheless, package it as they might, the simple words "object relations unit" brought with them to the United States an entire set of meanings and emotional nuances.

Rinsley (1978, 1982) described the historical and theoretical relationships among the all-good (rewarding) object relations unit, the all-bad (withdrawing) object relations unit, and the central ego and Fairbairn's libidinal, antilibidinal, and central object relations. Relying on Mahler's concepts, Rinsley showed that separation and individuation lead to integrating all-good and all-bad object relations into whole object relations, and to consolidating the central ego. He also acknowledged the contribution of Klein's ideas about the good and bad breast and the depressive position realization that the frustrating object is merely another aspect of the gratifying object. Without using the term *object relations unit*, Ogden (1986) described a similar process.

Kernberg (1976) seems to consider the self and object in object relations to be images or representations, rather like Jacobson's (1964) interpretation. He does not consider self-images autonomous, volitional, or self-reflective, although he points out how the self influences and changes those ego functions (Kernberg 1982). Kernberg's distinction answers the ego psychology criticism that some object relations theories seem to depict individuals as inhabited by various homunculi or as possessed by demons. He achieves clarity, however, by sacrificing the notion of people's subjective sense of feeling compelled by or identified with certain self-experiences. In extreme cases, borderline patients often feel that they are the self of their object relationship of the moment and completely overlook the fact that they feel and act otherwise at other times. For healthier individuals as well, self-image, as a representation, seems somewhat illusory, too dilute to describe a volitional personhood, especially since the sense of identity shifts a little from time to time.

Kernberg (1976) explicitly includes drive in his object relations units, unlike Fairbairn, who rejects the drive concept entirely and dismisses the id as a structural element. Fairbairn considers the id a concept suggesting a repository of disembodied drives, which he did not believe existed outside a relationship (1954). Consequently, Kernberg's formulation of object relations as self, affect-drive, and object at first sight seems to reintroduce drives into object relations. Were that the case, the drives and their subjective manifestation—affects—would bind self and object together and provide the cathexis, so to speak.

Attempting to integrate ego psychology and object relations, Kernberg retains the notion of drive while asserting that drives are always associated with self and object images. Self and object are in relationship. This emphasis approaches Fairbairn's solution of retaining libido, originally a term for erotic drive, as part of the concept of libidinal ego. More radically, however, Fairbairn retains the word libidinal and explicitly rejects a biological drive concept of the id and the disembodied libido (the noun) while retaining libidinal (the adjective).

Unlike Rinsley and Grotstein, Kernberg did not emphasize the similarity between his thinking and that of Fairbairn. Nevertheless he eventually changed his concept of drive to resemble Fairbairn's more than Freud's (1905b) or Anna Freud's (1936) ideas. He came to define drives as consolidations of affects, with affects always associated with self and object images (Kernberg 1982). Thus in Kernberg's thinking, emotions in relation to the self and others become primary while drives become secondary consolidations and manifestations of emotional relationships. This interpretation actually reverses the ego psychology and drive theory concept of instincts as preeminent, with both affects and relationships resulting from gratification or frustration of drive discharge.

As mentioned in previous chapters, Kernberg, by redefining drives, seems to have eliminated the concept from psychoanalytic thought. If drive means affect, not instinctual impulse, why call it drive? Although Greenberg and Mitchell (1983) correctly point out that Kernberg did not successfully reconcile the concept of drive with object relations theory, they may underestimate how successfully Kernberg's interpretation allowed U.S. ego psychologists to consider and begin to utilize contributions from object relations while retaining ego psychology terminology. Key among Kernberg's contributions is the understanding that affects and motivation are always paired with self and object, and that the concept previously called instinct is probably better considered a consolidation of affects or emotions that are personal, not impersonal, disembodied forces.

Self psychology (Kohut 1971), for its part, does not describe separate and opposite constellations in earliest mental life, but emphasizes the self as unitary from the beginning. Nevertheless, self psychology implies object relations patterns. The self relates to a sustaining self-object via empathy. The presence of a self-object is seen as necessary throughout life to maintain cohesiveness within the self. This formulation appears similar to object relations, although not so neatly packaged: self is always related to object by affect, in that empathy is an affective communication. Kohut thinks it impossible that an individual can exist outside a relationship, and he dispenses with the notions of both ego and drives. He does acknowledge the grandiose, idealizing, and mirroring transferences as evidence for common or primordial relationship patterns.

Daniel Stern's (1985) compilation of infant–parent physiological studies supports Kohut's conceptualization of the infant as originally cohesive, separate, and related, but dependent on parental emotional attunement and responsiveness to maintain cohesiveness in relation to others. Inevitable lapses in attunement cause self-fragmentation and polarization with which the individual and the objects must cope. Stern, unlike Kohut, describes the self–other experience of infants in "units," which he calls representations of interactions that have been generalized (RIGs). While providing a catchy acronym, he does not deny the complexity and fluidity of the unit concept. From a more cognitive and ego psychology viewpoint, Horowitz (1979, 1991, 1992) has empirically studied and described states of mind and person schemas in object relations.

All these approaches to object relations, with the exception of Horowitz's, seem to search for the primordial self–other relationship, seeking the essence of original, paradisiacal innocence, or perhaps the original, infantile problem of alienation or paradise lost, depending on the author's emphasis. Despite our supposed scientifically informed, philosophically up-to-date sophistication, we may retain a compelling need to seek the original innocence of tragic humankind or the original sin of guilty humankind. In fact, all of us are probably to some degree and at various times innocent, guilty, and tragic.

In *Self and Others* I described early childhood development in terms of primordial relationships. Relying heavily on Mahler's, Kernberg's, and Rinsley's works, I described the autistic phase of child development, followed by the dual unity of symbiosis, beginning separation-individuation, and split object relations evolving into integration, differentiation, and whole object relations. At the time of the book's second printing, I acknowledged that Stern's (1985) work casts grave doubts on the concept of autism as a phase. Now I am not at all sure that any of these phases unfolds smoothly and sequentially, although sketching some general patterns for use in parent guidance literature and for heuristic purposes perhaps is useful. People, even infants, seem to have many experiences of themselves in relation to others, along with the capacity to shift and blur who is self and who is object at times, through projection and introjection. Clinically, at least with adults, it seems more useful to study the various conscious and unconscious experiences patients have of themselves and others and what these experiences have to do with their memories, transference and countertransference, and current relationships than it does to search for ultimate or basic units of relatedness.

My work has moved farther from the concept of a single, driven self toward acknowledging the primacy of relationships from the beginning of life, without being certain what these relationships are or were. The kinds of experiences available to children probably vary in a more complex fashion than from single all-good to all-bad relationships or from a fragmented to a cohesive self. In working with adults, an infinite variety of object relations is clearly available, as indicated by Stern's (1985) concept of relationships that have been internalized and generalized or Horowitz's (1992) concept of states of mind. Even the relationship that Grotstein (1990) calls the abyss or the black hole of nothingness, while an unfortunate relationship of absence and perhaps the inverse of symbiotic unity, is still a relationship, and worth considering.

The search for an ideal of integrated adult health may be as futile as searching for the primordial relationship. Mature individuals may not have a single, balanced way of being with others: an ideal, mature ego, unflappable in its neutralized energy and modulated drive, may not exist. Even healthy adults seem to change their experiences of self in relation to others. Some such shifts have been discussed by Kohut (1971) in his emphasis of varying self-experience that depends on the availability of sustaining selfobjects; by Ogden (1986) in his description of the alternation between the schizoid and the depressive position throughout life; by Horowitz (1991) in his discussion of states of mind; by Grotstein (1994) in his comments on the aliveness of internal object relations throughout life; and by Gabbard (1994) in his assertion that the sense of self may be more variable in adult life than many people can comfortably acknowledge.

As Beahrs (1982) points out, describing relationship constellations as variable need neither imply that everyone has multiple personality or borderline fragmentation nor preclude the notion of an overarching sense of Self (Horowitz and Zilberg 1983) aware of all the variations. More mature and healthier individuals clearly have less dramatic and confusing shifts in self–other states and more integrated, nuanced, and complex senses of self. On the other hand, healthy persons may also vary in internal relationships more than is implied by an ideal of neutralized ego energy in the maturely "structured" individual. Such an ideal of stability may be excessively inhibited and closed against new experiences, new relationships, new and increasingly sophisticated senses of the self and others, and continued psychological, and perhaps spiritual, growth throughout life.

THE EGO

Freud (1923) used the term *ego* in highly variable ways. He employed the common German pronoun *Ich*, meaning "I" and "self." At different times ego can mean one's own person as seen by others, self-image, executive agency of the mind, the seat of personal will, or a structural element within the constellation id, ego, and superego. In his English *Standard Edition* of Freud's writings, Strachey (Freud 1923) translated *Ich* in a technical sense as "ego" and used "I," "me," and "self" for more everyday purposes. Although Freud used *ego* in many ways, his structural theory defined it as the executive agency of the mind, functioning both consciously and unconsciously to modulate id drive pressures, the superego's moral demands, and the exigencies of external reality.

Differentiation of ego as self- and as agency-structure awaited Hartmann's (1964) clarification. He emphasized the functions of differentiation, integration, synthesis, and balancing in the realms of perception, cognition, impulse control, movement, and the demands of conscience. He coined the term *autonomous ego function* for the neurophysiologically determined mental processes present from birth and not derived from id impulse turned back on itself. These "autonomous" ego functions have certain similarities to the mental processes studied in academic psychology, described in the mental status examination, and specified and standardized in neuropsychological tests. Hartmann gave the ego dynamic meaning and power, however, by retaining it within the constellation of id, ego, and superego and thereby taking into account unconscious conflict. Although he described ego as self-image, he did not focus on this personal self as much as on the executive functions (Allen 1977). His theory thereby became technical at the expense of the personal and subjective.

In her writings Jacobson (1964) reintroduced the importance of the self as an internal representation. She did not describe the self as having the power to decide and act: it remained an image created and perceived by the ego. Nevertheless, her emphasis on the ego's sense of personal self renewed the importance of the subjective and personal in ego psychology.

Kernberg (1976) gratefully acknowledges Jacobson's influence. As his ideas evolve, he comes to define the self as a supraordinate sum total of self-representations originating in the ego (Kernberg 1982). He seems to rely upon Hartmann's and Jacobson's definitions of system ego, with the addition of the idea of the self embedded in and reflexively influencing the ego. That is, while self is a structure in the ego, it also influences the ego functions, particularly of reality testing and maintaining object relations.

In writing about early development and primitive character structures, Kernberg emphasizes the self in object relations, not the ego in id-ego-superego. On the other hand, when writing about oedipal and postoedipal development and neurotic problems, he emphasizes the ego in tripartite structure—id, ego, and superego (Kernberg 1992). The necessity of this shift in focus from object relations structure (self, affect, object) to tripartite structure (id-ego-superego) is complexly argued. Although Kernberg calls the process of shifting *structuralization*, the reason for the shift from object relations concepts to tripartite concepts remains unclear aside from a possible loyalty to traditional ego psychology. An attempt to integrate object relations into ego functioning rather than the inverse—to integrate ego functioning into object relations—may be one factor contributing to Kernberg's theoretical shift when discussing more mature individuals.

Following Federn's (1952) lead, Rinsley (1982) describes ego feelings and internal and external ego boundaries. These concepts imply a subjective sense of self as well as ego function. Rinsley uses the words *ego* and *self* separately at times without actually distinguishing between them. He tends to use *self* in discussing object relations units and *ego* in other cases. For example, he discusses an alliance between the pleasure ego and the rewarding or all-good object relations unit, including the self. As the individual matures, the reality ego and the healthy, integrated, or whole object relations unit form an alliance that again includes the mature self. The pleasure ego, which he equates with Fairbairn's libidinal ego, becomes transformed into the reality ego, which he equates with Fairbairn's central ego. Rinsley seldom discusses traditional structural theory except to compare it to Fairbairn's thinking, which Rinsley seems to favor. Unlike Kernberg, he does not abandon object relations theory for structural theory at the oedipal phase.

Overlapping definitions of ego and self are ambiguous. Although gray areas and ambiguities exist in nature, theories are built on abstractions that artificially and temporarily limit vagueness so that clinicians and theoreticians alike can think clearly about various aspects of a problem or phenomenon. It does not seem wise to sacrifice clarity for comprehensiveness without careful consideration, even if Freud himself was unclear at times.

Ambiguity also allows for intellectual sleight of hand, which can conceal internal contradictions or conflicts with external data or competing theories. For example, ambiguity can obscure theoretical contradiction by creating an *appearance* of unity between ego psychology and object relations theory or self psychology rather than a true compatibility. Under such circumstances, the appearance of unity can hinder constructive attempts to deal with contradictions.

In *Self and Others* (1988) I followed Hartmann's and Jacobson's line of thinking a bit further by clearly distinguishing between ego and self. Any subjective sense pertaining to one's own person as opposed to an object was considered a sense of self. Even the notion of one's own ego was a self-image. The ego was "an abstraction denoting the set of mental functions of differentiation, integration, balancing, and organizing in the realms of perception, memory, cognition, emotions, actions and the demands of conscience" (pp. 28–29).

This clear distinction between ego and self, however, creates its own difficulties. A major problem is that the concept of observing ego becomes deprived of its reflexive sense (Hamilton 1988). Allen (1977) points out that such sharp distinctions provide no way to depict the thing observed and the thing observing as being the same. According to my former definition, people cannot observe their own ego functioning, only their self-representations. Clarity results in misrepresenting the subjective experience.

In addition to this metapsychological and terminological problem, clinical shortcomings arise from sharp theoretical separation of self and ego. Psychoanalysts and other psychotherapists observe that lack of a coherent sense of self is associated with pervasive ego function deficits (Kernberg 1975, Knight 1953). Conversely, patients with a flexible, overarching sense of self or identity usually also have more effective ego functioning in general. *Within* individuals over time, there seems to be a correspondence between self and ego functioning (Brown 1989) similar to the one observed *among* individuals.

There are clinical and theoretical difficulties with either clearly distinguishing self and ego or not distinguishing them. One way to solve this conundrum may be to include *ego functioning* along with *self, object,* and *affect-sensation* in a description of an organically whole state of mind or object relations constellation. Thus, *ego* and *self* are clearly differentiated terms, inherently related to one another. *Affect-sensation,* rather than *affect-drive,* seems the preferable term: both refer to feelings, the former emotional and the latter somatic, rather than to the nineteenth-century notion of drive. The term *drive* seems useful only in that it can refer to a subjective sense of feeling driven, that is, in that it refers to an affect or sensation.

OBJECT RELATIONS STATES

In a clinical theory, several advantages accrue from adding ego functioning to object relations, thereby creating object relations states as the central structural element. Such a theory defines ego and self clearly and separately, yet makes them related concepts. Clinically it provides a corrective for the exclusive focus on self currently prevalent in self psychology, but also common among those influenced by object relations theories, and adds specificity to the concept of self-fragmentation, which self psychologists use to describe episodes of disorganization, including cognitive disorganization.

Adding the ego as an element of object relations reintroduces into a primarily "relational/structural model" (Greenberg and Mitchell 1983, p. 407) the ego as a theoretical link to brain function, as

Hartmann (1964) originally suggested. Although clinicians sympathetic to Fairbairn's ideas may cogently argue that changes in what I call ego function are entirely explainable as related to the functioning self, adding the separate yet related concept of ego provides a terminology necessary to consider how changes in brain functioning may affect object relations, including the self-experience (Hamilton 1995). This approach does not attempt yet another integration of what Greenberg and Mitchell describe as the drive/structure model and relations/structure model. Instead, it adds one useful element from the drive/structure model to the relations/structure model: it adds ego, not drive, to object relations. By introducing the ego into relationships, rather than including relationships within ego, the theory remains clearly a relational/structure theory yet provides a framework for understanding brief or temporary shifts in ego functioning. The same framework describes preoedipal and postoedipal individuals, and thus provides theoretical and clinical parsimony.

There are certain drawbacks to this framework as with all theories. It is complex and requires thinking about multiple factors simultaneously, a clinically difficult feat. It depends on detailed technical definition, which detracts from the common, everyday language so important to the human interaction between patient and therapist. Furthermore, key assumptions have not yet been thoroughly tested or even discussed.

It is assumed that self, object, affect-sensation, and ego functioning shift in unison, a clinically observable phenomenon that can be validated or disconfirmed. Although examples of such shifts are provided in the foregoing chapters and in certain instances by Horowitz (1992), these few examples do not suffice. It is hypothesized here that shifting object relations are *always* accompanied by alterations in the state of ego functioning, just as Kernberg (1976) asserted that affects are always in relationship to self and object.

This phenomenon requires more systematic confirmation by clinical observation.

Another difficulty arises from the fact that the construct discussed in this book is incompatible with the long-held notion of id, ego, and superego as the structural unit in mature individuals and raises the possibility of replacing the tripartite model with a new structural psychology: self, affect-sensation, object, and ego functioning. The role of what has been termed superego has not been thoroughly discussed, although this new model contains within it the possibility of replacing superego with ego modulation of various preferred self-images (ego ideals) and sets of values concerning how people should treat one another. Just as the superego concept originally formulated by Freud (1923) cannot be entirely reconciled with Fairbairn's structural theory, neither can it be entirely reconciled with the theory presented here, because my approach provides a different understanding of how people think and feel and relate to one another. From my viewpoint, morality is not an abstract principle separate from relationships, but a set of experiences and expectations about how one should treat others, should be treated by others, and should treat oneself based on previous experiences with particular relationships and thoughts about those relationships.

To use an analogy from Judeo-Christian tradition, the morality prescribed by the Ten Commandments can be considered from a drive theory viewpoint, a set of abstract principles reluctantly internalized by a recalcitrant people who identify with a superior, ultimately powerful father whom they fear. From a relationship psychology viewpoint, the morality revealed at Mount Sinai is a personal covenant about the loving bond between God and humankind, the bond between God and the individual, God and the people, and among the people themselves. This morality is a set of relationship expectations derived from a relationship.

The difficulties of reconciling object relations theory with ego psychology are enhanced by an underlying assumption, presented in this book, that mature ego functioning, and consequently self-experience, varies more than most clinicians like to think (Gabbard 1994). This, too, is an observable phenomenon that has yet to be validated systematically.

CONCLUSION

This book opened with the clinical problem of retaining the useful ideas in ego psychology and reintroducing them into object relations theory. Pursuing this problem led to an application of object relations concepts to a larger clinical population than has previously been accepted. Along the way, the issue of conceptualizing people arose. Are people collections of mechanical forces and abstract regulating systems and structures? My approach shows that such a formula misses what is central to our humanness. People, as described in this book, are *always* in relationship. Our very humanness *is* our relationships. Each person is a self in relation to others, and ego functions become important only in that they play a part in those relationships.

The danger of dehumanizing patients arises when our theories become too mechanical. Nevertheless, the fact remains that we can be considered, and can consider ourselves, impersonally. One way to retain what is useful in impersonal thought systems, such as ego psychology, is to place these systems in the context of relationships, rather than to consider relationships as an epiphenomenon of impersonal systems. In this book, people are first and foremost in relation to others. Everything, including mental processes, must be considered within the context of these relationships.

Introducing ego functions into object relations, however, has unexpectedly led to the observation that ego functioning shifts with self–other relationships and affects. This rather uncomfortable, unsettling view of people, even mature people, as in such flux has led some authors to postulate a supraordinate Self (Horowitz and Zilberg 1983). Self is here considered always in relation to object. Thus we must also consider the possibility of a supraordinate Object when we accept the presence of a supraordinate Self.

Many questions remain unanswered. For now, perhaps it is enough to have contributed some thoughts on how people think and feel and behave in relation to the self and others, both internally and externally. Most psychodynamic theories have not attempted to become a general and complete psychology of the human mind (Freud 1914). Neither does my version of object relations theory and its therapeutic approaches claim completeness. I hope that it contributes some new ideas and approaches of interest and utility.

References

Adler, G. (1985). *Borderline Psychopathology and Its Treatment*. New York: Jason Aronson.

—— (1992). Psychotherapy of the narcissistic personality disordered patient: two contrasting approaches. In *From Inner Sources: New Directions in Object Relations Psychotherapy*, ed. N. G. Hamilton, pp. 195–212. Northvale, NJ: Jason Aronson.

Allen, J. G. (1977). Ego states and object relations. *Bulletin of the Menninger Clinic* 41:533–538.

Beahrs, J. O. (1982). *Unity and Multiplicity: Multilevel Consciousness of Self in Hypnosis, Psychiatric Disorder, and Mental Health*. New York: Brunner/Mazel.

Bion, W. R. (1962). *Learning from Experience*. London: Heinemann.

Brenner, C. (1973). *An Elementary Textbook of Psychoanalysis*, rev. ed. New York: International Universities Press.

Brown, L. J. (1989). A proposed demography of the representational world (revised version). Felix and Helene Deutsch Prize Paper. Boston Psychoanalytic Institute and Society.

Dewain, M. J. (1992). Adding medications to ongoing psychotherapy: indications and pitfalls. *American Journal of Psychotherapy* 46:102–110.

Fairbairn, W. R. D. (1943). The repression and the return of bad objects (with special reference to the "war neuroses"). In *Psychoanalytic Studies of the Personality*, London: Tavistock and Routledge & Kegan Paul, 1952.

—— (1954). *An Object Relations Theory of the Personality*. New York: Basic Books.

—— (1958). On the nature and aims of psychoanalytic treatment. *International Journal of Psycho-Analysis* 39:374–385.

—— (1963). Synopsis of an object-relations theory of the personality. *International Journal of Psycho-Analysis* 44:224–225.

Federn, P. (1952). *Ego Psychology and the Psychoses*. New York: Basic Books.

Freud, A. (1936). *The Ego and the Mechanisms of Defense*. New York: International Universities Press.

Freud, S. (1905a). Fragment of an analysis of a case of hysteria. *Standard Edition* 7:3–122.

—— (1905b). Three essays on the theory of sexuality. *Standard Edition* 7:136–243.

—— (1914). On the history of the psychoanalytic movement. *Standard Edition* 14:1–66.

—— (1923). The ego and the id. *Standard Edition* 19:3–66.

Gabbard, G. O. (1989). Splitting in hospital treatment. *American Journal of Psychiatry* 146:444–451.

—— (1994). *Psychodynamic Psychiatry in Clinical Practice: DSM-IV Edition*. Washington, DC: American Psychiatric Press.

Greenberg, J. R., and Mitchell, S. A. (1983). *Object Relations in Psychoanalytic Theory*. Cambridge, MA: Harvard University Press.

Greenson, R. R. (1971). The "real" relationship between the patient and the psychoanalyst. In *The Unconscious Today: Essays in Honor of Max Schur*, ed. M. Kanzer, pp. 213–232. New York: International Universities Press.

Grotstein, J. S. (1981). *Splitting and Projective Identification*. New York: Jason Aronson.

—— (1990). Nothingness, meaninglessness, chaos, and the "black hole": I. Meaninglessness, nothingness, and chaos. *Contemporary Psychoanalysis* 26:257–290.

—— (1994). Endopsychic structure and the cartography of the internal world: six endopsychic characters in research of an author. In *Fairbairn and the Origins of Object Relations*, ed. J. S. Grotstein and D. B. Rinsley, pp. 174–194. New York: Guilford.

Grotstein, J. S., and Rinsley, D. B., eds. (1994). *Fairbairn and the Origins of Object Relations*. New York: Guilford.

Guntrip, H. J. S. (1969). *Schizoid Phenomena, Object Relations and the Self*. New York: International Universities Press.

Hamilton, N. G. (1988). *Self and Others: Object Relations Theory in Practice*. Northvale, NJ: Jason Aronson.

—— (1989). A critical review of object relations theory. *American Journal of Psychiatry* 146:1552–1560.

—— (1990). The containing function and the analyst's projective identification. *International Journal of Psycho-Analysis* 71: 445–453.

——, ed. (1992a). *From Inner Sources: New Directions in Object Relations Psychotherapy*. Northvale, NJ: Jason Aronson.

—— (1992b). Splitting and projective identification among healthier individuals. In *From Inner Sources: New Directions in Object Relations Psychotherapy*, ed. N. G. Hamilton, pp. 85–97. Northvale, NJ: Jason Aronson.

—— (1994). Object relations theory. In *Encyclopedia of Human Behavior*, vol. 3, ed. V. S. Ramachandran, pp. 321–332. San Diego: Academic Press.

—— (1995). Object relations units and the ego. *Bulletin of the Menninger Clinic*. 59:416–426.

Hamilton, N. G., Sacks, L. H., and Hamilton, C. A. (1994). Object relations theory and pharmacopsychotherapy of anxiety disorders. *American Journal of Psychotherapy* 48:380–391.

Hartmann, H. (1964). *Ego Psychology and the Problem of Adaptation.* New York: International Universities Press.

Horowitz, M. J. (1979). *States of Mind.* New York: Plenum.

——, ed. (1991). *Person Schemas and Maladaptive Interpersonal Patterns.* Chicago: University of Chicago Press.

—— (1992). Formulation of states of mind. In *From Inner Sources: New Directions in Object Relations Psychotherapy,* ed. N. G. Hamilton, pp. 75–97. Northvale, NJ: Jason Aronson.

Horowitz, M. J., and Zilberg, N. (1983). Regressive alterations of the self concept. *American Journal of Psychiatry* 140:284–289.

Jacobson, E. (1964). *The Self and the Object World.* New York: International Universities Press.

Karasu, T. B. (1992). The worst of times, the best of times. *Journal of Psychotherapy Practice and Research* 1:2–15.

Kernberg, O. F. (1975). *Borderline Conditions and Pathological Narcissism.* New York: Jason Aronson.

—— (1976). *Object Relations Theory and Clinical Psycho-Analysis.* New York: Jason Aronson.

—— (1982). Self, ego, affects, and drives. *Journal of the American Psychoanalytic Association* 30:893–917.

—— (1984). *Severe Personality Disorders: Psychotherapeutic Strategies.* New Haven: Yale University Press.

—— (1992). An ego psychology–object relations theory approach to the transference. In *From Inner Sources: New Directions in Object Relations Psychotherapy,* ed. N. G. Hamilton, pp. 29–51. Northvale, NJ: Jason Aronson.

King, P. H. M. (1983). The life and work of Melanie Klein in the British Psycho-Analytical Society. *International Journal of Psycho-Analysis* 64:251–260.

Klein, M. (1932). *The Psycho-Analysis of Children.* London: Hogarth.

—— (1946). Notes on some schizoid mechanisms. *International Journal of Psycho-Analysis* 27:99–110.

Klein, M., and Riviere, J. (1964). *Love, Hate, and Reparation.* New York: W. W. Norton.

Knight, R. P. (1953). Borderline states. *Bulletin of the Menninger Clinic* 17:1–12.

Kohut, H. (1971). *The Analysis of the Self.* New York: International Universities Press.

—— (1977). *The Restoration of the Self.* New York: International Universities Press.

Langs, R. (1980). *Interactions: The Realm of Transference and Countertransference.* New York: Jason Aronson.

Lewy, A. J., Sack, R. L., Miller, L. S., and Hoban, T. M. (1987). Antidepressant and circadian phase shifting effects of light. *Science* 235:352–354.

Lichtenberg, J., Bornstein, M., and Silver, D. (1984). *Empathy,* vols. I and II. Hillsdale, NJ: Analytic Press.

Mahler, M. S., Pine, F., and Bergman, A. (1975). *The Psychological Birth of the Human Infant.* New York: Basic Books.

Masterson, J. F. (1976). *Psychotherapy of the Borderline Adult: A Developmental Approach.* New York: Brunner/Mazel.

Masterson, J. F., and Rinsley, D. B. (1975). The borderline syndrome: the role of the mother in the genesis and psychic structure of the borderline personality. *International Journal of Psycho-Analysis* 56:163–177.

Modell, A. H. (1968). *Object Love and Reality: An Introduction to a Psychoanalytic Theory of Object Relations.* New York: International Universities Press.

—— (1994). Fairbairn's structural theory and the communication of affects. In *Fairbairn and the Origins of Object Relations,* ed. J. S. Grotstein and D. B. Rinsley, pp. 195–207. New York: Guilford.

Ogden, T. H. (1982). *Projective Identification and Psychotherapeutic Technique.* New York: Jason Aronson.

—— (1986). *The Matrix of the Mind: Object Relations and the Psychoanalytic Dialogue.* Northvale, NJ: Jason Aronson.

—— (1994). The concept of internal object relations. In *Fairbairn and the Origins of Object Relations,* ed. J. S. Grotstein and D. B. Rinsley, pp. 88–111. New York: Guilford.

Rinsley, D. B. (1978). Borderline psychopathology: a review of aetiology, dynamics and treatment. *International Review of Psycho-Analysis* 5:45–54.

—— (1982). *Borderline and Other Self Disorders*. New York: Jason Aronson.

—— (1987). A reconsideration of Fairbairn's "original object" and "original ego" in relation to borderline and other self disorders. In *The Borderline Patient*, vol. 1, ed. J. S. Grotstein, M. F. Solomon, and J. A. Lang, pp. 219–232. Hillsdale, NJ: Analytic Press.

Robinson, R. G. (1995). Mapping brain activity associated with emotion. *American Journal of Psychiatry* 152:327–329.

Rubens, R. L. (1994). Fairbairn's structural theory. In *Fairbairn and the Origins of Object Relations*, ed. J. S. Grotstein and D. B. Rinsley, pp. 151–173. New York: Guilford.

Scharff, J. S., and Scharff, D. E. (1992). *Scharff Notes: A Primer of Object Relations Therapy*. Northvale, NJ: Jason Aronson.

Segal, H. (1964). *Introduction to the Work of Melanie Klein*. New York: Basic Books.

Stern, D. N. (1985). *The Interpersonal World of the Infant: A View from Psychoanalysis and Developmental Psychology*. New York: Basic Books.

Stolorow, R. D., Brandchaft, B., and Atwood, G. E. (1992). Intersubjectivity in psychoanalytic treatment. In *From Inner Sources: New Directions in Object Relations Psychotherapy*, ed., N. G. Hamilton, pp. 181–193. Northvale, NJ: Jason Aronson.

Sullivan, H. S. (1953). *The Interpersonal Theory of Psychiatry*. New York: W. W. Norton.

Sutherland, J. D. (1989). *Fairbairn's Journey into the Interior*. London: Free Association Books.

Symington, N. (1994). The tradition of Fairbairn. In *Fairbairn and the Origins of Object Relations*, ed. J. S. Grotstein and D. B. Rinsley, pp. 211–221. New York: Guilford.

Tolpin, M. (1971). On the beginnings of a cohesive self: an application of the concept of transmuting internalization in the study of the transitional object and signal anxiety. *Psychoanalytic Study of the Child* 26:316–352. New Haven, CT: Yale University Press.

Wallerstein, R. S., ed. (1992). *The Common Ground of Psychoanalysis.* Northvale, NJ: Jason Aronson.

Winnicott, D. W. (1949). Hate in countertransference. *International Journal of Psycho-Analysis* 30:69–74.

—— (1953). Transitional objects and transitional phenomena: a study of the first not-me possession. *International Journal of Psycho-Analysis* 34:89–97.

—— (1965). *The Maturational Processes and the Facilitating Environment.* New York: International Universities Press.

—— (1968). *The Family and Individual Development.* London: Tavistock.

Index